Beyond the Next Mountain

BEYOND THE NEXT MOUNTAIN

By

Mawii Pudaite

Accelerated Christian Education,® Inc.
Lewisville, Texas

All Scripture references are taken from the
King James Version of the Bible, unless
otherwise noted.

ISBN 1-56265-019-X

2 3 4 5 6   Printing/Year   05 04 03 02 01 00

Printed in the United States of America

This book is
lovingly dedicated
to my children

Paul Rozarlien
John Lalnunsang
Mary Lalsangpui

who are the pride
and joy of our hearts
and through whom
Rochunga and I
have learned
so much of God
and His eternal love
and purposes.

CONTENTS

ACKNOWLEDGMENTS

A project such as this needs special acknowledgments to many people who assisted with an effort that has been several years in development.

I am grateful to Kenneth Bliss of Inspirational Films who suggested the idea that I write a book to go with the motion picture based on my husband's life. Ken felt that such a book could have a life of its own beyond that of the film.

The material, of course, originated with Rochunga, the masterful storyteller. No book can do justice to his unique storytelling ability, but for those unable to hear him speak firsthand, perhaps this manuscript can share some of his personality.

Thanks are also expressed to Jim and Marti Hefley, Ro's biographers, who told his story in the book *God's Tribesman*, and to other research which added to the background of this project. In this regard, contributions of James Collier, Lee Roddy, and Rolf Forsberg are gratefully acknowledged.

My deep and abiding gratitude must also be expressed to my beloved parents (who are now with the Lord) and my older brothers and sisters in northeast India. This book is one tangible result of their sacrificial commitment—they gave so unselfishly in order that I would receive an education. Such unconditional love has sustained me in so many ways and in so many hours.

And without continuing encouragement from our dear friend Dr. Ken Taylor, and the guidance of Tyndale's editor-in-chief, Wendell Hawley, and the editing of Vicki deVries, the book would not have become reality.

I am especially grateful to the Lord for how he brought writer Joe Musser to us. Since he first met Ro nearly fifteen years ago, they have been teamed for God's purposes. If anyone is qualified to write about Ro, it is Joe, whose friendship with my husband is very much like that of David and Jonathan.

Joe and I have worked on this project together with a freshness that has come from the Lord. Both of us have heard Ro's stories many times, but we are always just as spellbound as ever. Each telling has a power and a reality that never fail to transform listening audiences. Just as Ro's stories point people to the Savior he seeks to glorify, it is our prayer that this book will have a similar ministry.

As you read it, it is our prayer that you say—as missionary Watkin Roberts says later in this story—"What an amazing Christ!" If you catch a glimpse of our wonderful Savior, our prayers for this project will have been answered.

Mawii Pudaite
Wheaton, Illinois

Chawnga being beaten for refusing to stop preaching the gospel to his people. Scene from the film *Beyond the Next Mountain*, an Inspirational Films release

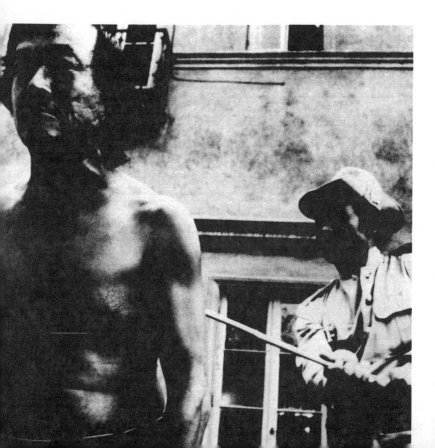

INTRODUCTION

Centuries ago our people, the Hmars, came from the north—from China—in what must have been waves of migrations from beyond the Himalayan ridges—from China's plains. There are stories of how a great famine caused our ancestors to travel south to Manipur, through the difficult passes in the mountains our people named *Himalawi* and the British white men called *Himalayas.* Our state of Manipur, in northeast India, is one of the most beautiful parts not only in India but in all the world.

The land of the Hmars is located deep in the heart of a strange geological stretch of jungles and mountains. No snow ever falls on its highest peaks although most mountains at 7,000 feet have mantles of white. The jungle area is a vast, almost impenetrable forest in the valleys, but the trees surrounding the valleys grow at an elevation of several thousand feet above sea level, close to the tops of the soaring mountain peaks. A myriad of dangers may be found in the jungle area—wild bears and the infamous Royal Bengal man-eating tigers, to name a few.

The Hmars have oriental features in contrast to the neighboring Hindus and Bengalis. However, we have no recorded history because we have never had a written language. Only stories told by grandfather to grandson were passed along.

Spirit worship and the fear which accompanied it were the way of our people. Our grandfathers and their forebears were convinced they had been told by spirits that the enemy whose head was cut off would be one's slave in the next world. The spirits would be greatly angered if a pig or chicken were not sacrificed to them. On rare occasions, even a human might be sacrificed.

Our people never thought of themselves as savages. Violence was but a small part of their heritage. For the most part, the men of the Hmar tribe of northeast India consisted of hunters, planters, storytellers, and musicians. The women took care of the needs of their husbands and children; their duties included weaving, cooking, and carrying wood and water.

The warriors, who were also the headhunters, did not take heads in unprovoked attacks. Only in battle was it proper to cut off the head of an enemy. Buola, the father of Chawnga, was a leader of the Hmars. He was famous among our people for his bravery. The heads of many enemies decorated the *sawngka* (open porch) of his bamboo house.

A hundred years ago the British, who took our land, considered us ignorant and bloodthirsty savages. The Hmars had known little of the red-coated, white-faced soldiers. For the most part the British settled in India, and technically our area was part of the northeast frontier area, a buffer zone between the rest of India and Burma.

Without the knowledge or consent of the Hmars, the British colonial government secretly annexed their land and gave it to a local *rajah*. The land was cleared and countless tea plantations were created. Assam tea was in great demand around the world, and the need for more and more tea plantations became a pressing issue to the British.

The Hmar hill tribes resented this subjection to outside rule. They demonstrated their feelings by frequent raids against British settlements or their agents.

In the days when Buola was a boy, the Hmars joined

forces with the Lushai tribe and attacked the British settlement at Cachar District. With spear and *dao* (machetelike blade) the warriors swarmed down onto the Alexanderpur tea plantation. Hundreds of workers were killed and their heads taken. The massacre was subdued when General Lord Frederick Roberts led colonial troops into the hills to avenge the killings and bring order to the tribe.

British rule was firmly established by the time Buola's son Chawnga was a boy. Chawnga enjoyed a fine heritage since his father was a man of prestige. Hmar men followed one of three basic occupations. They were warriors or farmers or hunters. A few, such as Chawnga's father, were proficient in all three. Buola was known publicly as a *thangsuo* ("famous one"). He was honored with a village celebration, given the *tawmlairang* (special feathered headgear) and *puondum* ("cloth of respect") to wear. The honor, according to the priest of the village, insured that Buola would go to *Pielral* (Paradise).

The house of Buola was one of the largest in the village. As was the custom, Buola's sons lived with him, along with their wives and children, and so did his slaves.

Slavery was common among the hill tribes. Widows and orphans, who were unable to support themselves, worked for food and shelter. Criminals could escape public trials and sentences by appealing to the sanctuary of a chief's house. If the wrongdoer stayed inside the chief's house and served, he was safe. But if he left the sanctuary, the criminal was at the mercy of his victim or victim's family.

Some slaves voluntarily indentured themselves during times of acute poverty or famine. But most slaves were bond servants, captured as the spoils of war. Unlike the voluntary slaves, these had no status; they were bought and sold as quickly and easily as pigs and chickens.

Often, when a *lal* (chief) died, his slaves were buried alive with him—to serve him in the world to come, along with the spirits of those whose heads the *lal* had taken.

The Hmars did not observe precise calendars. They marked

years by the cycle of seasons—winter, spring, summer, and autumn. Winter was the cold season, the time of light frosts at night although the days were warm. Usually it did not rain in winter. It was the time to harvest the rice and have a harvest celebration. Late winter was the time to assign plots for *jhums* (small farms). The jungle would be chopped and cleared, and the debris would be piled high to dry out for a month. Men, women, and children all turned out to help.

Spring was the season of sun and storms. The brush would be burned on the *jhums*, and the ashes raked into the soil. The seeds would then be sown, in time for the spring rains to water them.

Summer was noted for its monsoons. It was a hot, humid season, a time when life slowed for the tribe.

In autumn the rains stopped. The fields were weeded. Birds were chased from the *jhums*, where grain was ripening. But autumn was often treacherous. After the farmers had worked the fields and nurtured the crops, a storm would sometimes come, bringing terrible hail. The hailstones were frequently the size of hen's eggs and could completely destroy fields of grain in a matter of minutes. Floods, monsoons, drought, and hail were the common enemies of the Hmar farmer and were the most typical causes of famine in the hills.

After the crops were planted and the fields weeded, the farmers awaited the harvest. There was little else to do.

In this setting, so lush with greenery and so fertile for seed sowing, Chawnga—the father of my husband, Rochunga Pudaite—encountered the life-changing Word of God and the message of salvation. In this setting Rochunga and I would also come to know the Creator God and find the source of our greatest joy and blessing. From our simple jungle life, God would take us around the world in a mission dedicated to spreading his Word throughout the globe. It is a journey which is still going on. It is a true story which is still being lived. . . .

ONE
SO GREAT A CLOUD
OF WITNESSES

"Watkin Roberts has gone to be with the Lord." The reality of the death of this man whom my people, the Hmars, had called *Pu Tlangval* ("Mr. Young Man") slowly sunk in. It was hard to believe that "Dad" had now gone to his final reward. His pioneer missionary work in the hills of Manipur in northeast India had reaped many souls for Christ's Kingdom. He would be missed very much.

My husband, Rochunga—Ro, for short—seemed unusually quiet when we returned from the funeral held in Toronto. He and Roberts had come to be very close during the last ten years before Roberts' death. Partnership Mission, formerly called the Indo-Burma Pioneer Mission by Roberts, had been turned over to Ro's leadership. Three thousand children had already been given food, shelter, clothing, and education through the funds provided by donors from America. Ro's work had provided many churches, national missionaries, schools, and homeless children spiritual and financial support.

"Why are you so depressed?" I asked Ro. I knew Roberts' death had something to do with his down mood, but there was something else eating at my husband's usually cheerful outlook.

"It all seems so hopeless," Ro sighed. "How can one man make a difference even if he does much? Yes, if you look at what we have done in ten years, it seems remarkable. I don't intend to demean the Lord for what has been accomplished. What depresses me is looking at the entire picture."

"What do you mean?" I asked.

"Well, we now have only some 300 missionaries in India."

"Yes. . . ."

"That number can't keep pace with the birthrate in India!" Ro sighed. "I figured it out. It would take *4,000* missionaries *1,000 years* just to speak to everyone in India about Jesus just *one time!* Provided the population grows no more than one million a month. The Great Commission is an *impossible* task."

My stomach knotted as if I had just heard heresy. "But we cannot question God's words," I protested gently. "Think about all that the Lord has done through you already!"

We had seen the physical and spiritual restoration of many lives in the ten years of successful mission work. We could not discount those miracles. Ro's entire life, in fact, had been an unfolding miracle, spreading out like the ever expanding horizon. How far *had* the horizon taken him? From jungle boy to educated man on a mission for God.

"Think about what the Lord has done for you already, Ro," I repeated. "That will encourage you to think more optimistically about the future." He seemed lost in thought, so I quietly left him to meditate on my words and on the past through which God had guided him and our people. . . .

Ro began thinking about the lush hills of Manipur. In his mind's eye, he saw his father, Chawnga, telling him the story of the time when Mr. Young Man had come to his village of Senvon. . . .

. . . . Fifteen-year-old Chawnga was proud of his new status as a man of the village. No longer would he have to carry firewood as he had been doing since age six. Chawnga now lived in the *buonzawl* (bachelors' quarters where all un-

married men at the age of puberty were required to sleep).
The *buonzawl*, a combination of warrior training, school,
and community service, exerted a strong influence on the
village and tribal life. Usually the strict discipline imposed
by the *valupa* (youth commander) kept the young men in
line.

They hunted, sang around the fires at night, and shared
stories and jungle fables. Sometimes a bamboo house in
the village would catch on fire, and they would battle the
flames and put out the fire. Later, they might also assist the
hapless owner to rebuild the house.

Like the other teenagers, Chawnga could now hunt with
a gun instead of a snare or sling. No one remembers how
the Hmars learned how to make guns or gunpowder. Their
guns were unlike the deadly breech-loading ones of the
British, who used cartridges and could shoot many times
—the Hmars wrestled with muzzle-loading weapons.
Yet, though the Hmar firearms were crude, they were terrible and effective. They could bring down bears, tigers, or
elephants and just as easily, a man. The rifles were crafted
by the village blacksmith. Hmars made their own gunpowder. Young boys were taught early in life how to make it,
and Chawnga had done it many times.

Chawnga placed a screen of woven bamboo under the
chicken roost to catch hen droppings. Next, he made another screen—this time three layers of bamboo—to strain
the mixture when water was poured over the manure into a
huge pot. For a full day Chawnga boiled the mixture of
water and hen droppings, then finally poured what was left
of the cooked residue onto a large clay platter. During the
night, the mixture separated. A yellow, bubbling, gooey
substance made of nitrate settled on top, much the way
grease coagulates on top of soup after it cools.

The next day Chawnga went to the jungle to search out a
khawngma, which the Hmars called the "fiery tree." He
took some deadwood and made a fire. Once the flames
charred the wood, Chawnga doused it with the water he

had carried in the bamboo tubes. When the fire was out and the charcoal dry, he returned to the village with the charcoal and began the slow process of crushing it into powder with a wooden mortar.

Finally, Chawnga mixed the yellow nitrate with the charcoal powder. The recipe was not precise, but he knew how to test it. Holding a small amount in his hand, he sparked it. If it ignited readily without burning his hand, Chawnga knew it was ready.

The next morning Chawnga and a few of his friends went into the jungle to hunt. Buola gave Chawnga his own gun to use.

The mists still hung heavy over the mountains by the time of the midday meal. The young men sat quietly, each eating a handful of cooked rice wrapped in a big leaf. Monkeys chattered noisily in the trees above them, drowning out the songbirds. Chawnga smiled and nodded toward the treetops. His friends understood and nodded in return.

The monkeys were the watchdogs of the jungle. Their screams of alarm alerted the rest of the jungle when hunters were noisy or careless. The Hmar friends were still unnoticed by the monkeys. Their sounds were the shouts of play, not danger.

Perhaps they could surprise a bear or wild boar. To kill such a trophy would bring them recognition back at the village. Chawnga's three friends carried spears. They would have to get very close to an animal in order to kill it. There was danger in getting that near to a bear or boar.

The four young men crept silently through the jungle. It was dense and dark. Even when the sun burned through the fog and mists, it barely penetrated the foliage. Teak, mangrove, mahogany, oaks, and pines grew in abundance in the forest. But here, the jungle was lush with cane, vines, and bamboo. There were clumps of elephant bamboo nearly a hundred feet tall. Little wonder the Hmars worshiped nature.

The hills of Manipur were beautiful. The jungle forests

were like jade jewels set in the crown of the mountains. The valleys had green fields and transparent blue lakes, fed by rushing, clear mountain streams. Chawnga had often heard his father call their land "the jewel of India."

"That is why we fought the British when they gave our land to the Rajah," Buola had told him.

Tribal legends had prophesied the coming of the white man. A Hmar wise man over a century earlier had foretold that men with white skins would come and conquer the land with guns. The prophet added a cryptic footnote, however. He said the white-faced warriors would be followed by others who would tell of a new religion, one not requiring the sacrifice of pigs and chickens. No one in the tribe could imagine such a thing, however. The priests warned that the spirits would be angered by any change in religion. Yet, the first part of the prophecy had been accurate. . . .

Just now, however, the young hunters were not thinking about tribal legends. Chawnga spotted fresh tracks in the mud beside a stream. They were the unmistakable cloven footprints of a wild boar. Steam was still rising from fresh droppings nearby. Chawnga's heart skipped with excitement. They were close.

He cocked his ear to listen. There was a faint rustle in the brush some yards away. Then he heard it—the contented grunt of a wild sow grazing on roots and mushrooms.

Chawnga motioned to his friends and alerted them. With spears poised, they separated. Spreading out, they planned to encircle the boar and trap it in a small clearing for the kill.

Slowly and quietly they moved closer to the sounds. Chawnga held his breath, not wanting to betray their presence in any way.

Suddenly the jungle came alive with the frightened screams of monkeys. Chawnga froze. What had caused their alarm? None of the hunters had made any noise. Then he heard the enraged squeal of the boar, followed by the crashing sounds of its charge through the jungle underbrush.

Chawnga caught only a glimpse of animal as it rushed away toward the dark jungle, too quickly for him to get his gun up. Angrily Chawnga watched the tall grass rustle and then hide the quarry. He knew it would be impossible to pick up the trail if it got away now.

Then Chawnga heard a yell. His friend, Bumpu, had been close to where the boar charged. Bumpu stood firm and pushed his spear deeply into the chest of the boar. With a frenzied squeal, the big animal stumbled, tried to get up, and fell again—the spear had struck its heart. Blood gushed profusely from the wound as Chawnga and the others ran up to assist in the kill and congratulate Bumpu.

In a moment they slit the throat to hasten the bleeding and gutted the animal. Bumpu took his *dao* and, with a quick blow, swung down on the animal's neck. The head rolled off and was then retrieved. Bumpu stuck it on the spear as a trophy to carry back to the village.

"We should kill all those monkeys for nearly robbing us of our trophy," Bumpu muttered quietly.

Chawnga nodded, but looked toward the treetops. "What frightened them? They still do not know we are here," he whispered.

It was true. The cries of alarm were not in response to the Hmar hunters stalking the wild boar.

The chatter and squeals had come from a short distance— at the edge of the jungle where the grassy plain touched the forest. The monkeys had reacted to something coming from the mountains.

Chawnga put up his hand to silence his companions. They listened. There was only monkey chatter. No. There was something else.

The young men strained to hear, their faces wrinkled in frowns. It was a strange sound. A man's voice? Yes, but he was calling, or was it singing? But who would sing on the mountain? And why would someone be coming from the direction of the morning sun?

"Guide me, O Thou Great Jehovah," the white man sang

at the top of his lungs, "pilgrim through this wondrous land. I am weak, but Thou art mighty. Hold me in Thy powerful hand."

The guide named Dala walked in front of Roberts. Taisena and Savawma, the other escorts, followed behind Roberts with baggage. They stopped for a moment. The white man removed his pith helmet and wiped perspiration from his face.

"We are watched," Dala said.

"Where?" the white man asked. "I don't see anyone."

"They are there," Dala replied. "We cannot see them, but they know we are here."

Chawnga climbed into a large mangrove tree for a look. Faraway on the mountain he saw something—a man. No, four men. Three of the men were tribals, probably Lushais, judging from the colors of their *puons* (tribal loincloths). But the fourth man was not a Lushai. Could it even be said that he was a man? Chawnga had never seen a creature such as this one before. He was as tall as the tallest Hmar.

Chawnga watched as the men came closer, especially the tall, strange one dressed in unusual clothing. As he drew nearer, Chawnga could hear the man more clearly. He *was* singing. But in a language Chawnga could not understand.

Now Chawnga could see his face. The men had paused to rest. The Lushai guides looked around warily. The strange one took off a wide-brimmed hat to wipe his brow. The man had thick black hair like his own and dark flashing eyes, but Chawnga gasped to see his white skin.

A shudder went through Chawnga's body. His father, Buola, had told him many stories about the white skins called *British*. They had come earlier to the Assam and Manipur hills to conquer and kill when Buola was a boy.

But Chawnga had never seen a white man. Who was he? Was he a warrior? Were other soldiers following?

Chawnga quickly hurried to the others. The four Hmars decided to check more closely. If the strangers were alone, they could easily ambush and kill them, perhaps take their heads as trophies. And if there were others, they would find out and hurry back to the village and alert the tribe. More warriors would be needed if soldiers were coming.

TWO
BLOOD COVENANT

Nearing the edge of the jungle, the white man and his natives began to follow a path from a small stream leading directly to the Hmar village. Suddenly one of Chawnga's friends let out a chilling war cry. Then the warrior jumped out from the bushes, threw a spear in their direction, and ran back into the jungle.

The spear had been meant as a warning. Otherwise, at such close range, it would have hit the intended target. It quivered in the ground only inches in front of the white man.

"Tell them we mean them no harm. We are brothers. We come as friends," the white man instructed his guide.

"*Chibai! Chibai!*" ("Greetings! Greetings!") the guide called out, adding a few phrases in the Lushai language which the white man understood. Then the guide shouted also in Hmar.

Chawnga and his friends had by now warned the villagers of the imminent arrival of the strangers. They then circled back in time to see the white man entering a clearing. The jungle air was hot and humid. The white man's singing had stopped. Suddenly Chawnga and the three warriors ran across the clearing ahead of the intruders. Up ahead lay the village, similar to many villages in the state of Manipur.

The sound of drums could be heard coming from the village. Then a score of warriors with spears and *daos* (machetelike blades) began assembling to greet the white man and his guide.

When still out of spear-throwing range, the guide called out for Lal Kamkholun, the chief of the village, and explained the purpose of the visit. A muscular man approached warily.

"I am Lal Kamkholun," he said in Hmar.

"I have brought the man who sent you the book," the guide replied.

"No, it cannot be," the chief argued. "Such a book should come only from the hands of an old man, a wise man who has traveled from the outside world—from the land of white faces."

Forty Hmar warriors circled the strangers cautiously.

"I am your brother," the white man told the guide to say. "I come to bring you God's book. I will tell you its meaning. I have an offering of peace from God."

"Can such wisdom come from one with so few years?" the chief asked.

"It is God's wisdom. He speaks from this book. I am only his servant," the white man said. He held out his hand in a gesture of friendship. "My name is Watkin Roberts of Wales."

Lal Kamkholun frowned. He could not make out the sound of such strange words. "We will call you *Pu Tlangval* ('Mr. Young Man')," he said simply.

The Hmars conferred for a while, then told Watkin Roberts of their decision. He could stay.

For the next five days, the missionary lived as one of the tribesmen, sleeping in the *buonzawl* bamboo home with the unmarried men of the village. He ate steamed rice and talked of the Creator God and the words contained in the Bible he'd brought.

Roberts experienced difficulty with some of the Hmar beliefs. They rarely used their own names or spoke another's name because they feared the evil spirits would gain control if they knew the real name of a person. But Roberts convinced the Hmars that Jesus was stronger than evil, and so the tribesmen could "give their names to Jesus."

The missionary also learned that the natives had a curious custom of making peace with one another. When a tribal war had stretched on to where one or the other side was ready for peace, a chieftan might send an emissary to the other warring chief. The second chief's representative would meet and talk terms.

If the two were ready to negotiate peace, the chief would send a warrior at sunrise to beat a war drum three times from a hilltop adjacent to the enemy land. If the other tribe's war drum sounded the same note before nightfall, the chiefs would gather their elders and warriors and meet at the boundary line between their two tribes.

An animal would be sacrificed on the site. The two chiefs would discuss the terms of the agreement while the blood flowed across the boundary line. After the agreement was finalized, the two chiefs would embrace. The blood covenant was one which could not be broken.

Roberts told them in Lushai, "That was how God met man. God and man were at war. No man obeyed God's laws. There was no peace. But in making the sacrifice of blood for peace, God gave his own Son, Jesus."

The Hmar tribesmen were deeply impressed. They understood that kind of reconciliation.

After five days of in-depth communication with exposure to the Lushai translations of the Scripture portions, five young Hmars "gave their names to Jesus." One of them was Chawnga, son of Buola.

Then Mr. Young Man had to leave. He had already defied the authorities by coming to Senvon village. Staying there would compromise his missionary efforts completely. He might even be expelled from India if he did not return to the Lushai town of Aizawl, where he had been living for the past several months.

"I must leave," he said to Chawnga.

There was no mistaking Chawnga's disappointment. "But you cannot go yet! We want to know more about Creator God and his Son, Jesus."

The missionary also felt the frustration of leaving so soon. Five converts—with no Bible in their own language, no church, no experienced elders to nurture them in the faith. But he had no choice. If he stayed, he'd be either imprisoned or expelled.

"I am reminded of one of God's servants, the Apostle Paul," Roberts explained. "He said, 'I planted, but someone else will water, and another will harvest.' Somehow, God in his mercy—will not abandon you. God will care for you himself."

"But how can it be?" Chawnga asked. "We are not learned in the ways of Creator God."

"There is a school—a mission school. You can come and learn to read and write the Lushai language. More of the Bible will be translated for you in Lushai."

"Can we not learn God's ways from a book in the Hmar language?" Chawnga asked.

"But you have no written language," Roberts reminded him. "Someone from your tribe must study and give you the book in your language."

The missionary and his native guides left the next morning. A company of Hmars escorted them as far as the mountain of the morning sun, then said their sad good-byes.

THREE
PREACHER ON THE MOUNTAIN

Chawnga and the other four converts from the Hmar tribe did follow the ways of Jesus. They traveled regularly to Aizawl for training under Watkin Roberts (Mr. Young Man). Roberts had begun a missionary organization, *Thado-Kuki Pioneer Mission*, which he later changed to Northeast India General Mission. Its purpose was to bring Christianity to the northeast frontier of India and to the Burmese border area.

Then, explaining his concept of evangelism—nationals telling nationals—Roberts sent them back to their own village, as well as to neighboring ones to share the gospel of Jesus Christ.

Without the benefit of experienced Christian leadership—or even of a Bible in their own tongue, the five young Hmars were faithful to the missionary's admonition. They preached to their people, creating practical sermons out of the stories and activities of the people. Chawnga used the well-known prophecy and legend about the coming of the white men:

"You have heard how a wise man said long ago, in the days of our ancestors, that the white faces would come with guns. And they came. Our fathers have seen them. But do you not also remember the wise man said that other white faces would come and tell us of a new religion? I have met the white missionary called 'Mr. Young Man.' He told me about the one true path to seek and find the Creator God. It is this God whom we must worship. We must put aside our worship of nature and our sacrifices to evil spirits, just as the wise man told us. We must find peace with Creator God and get forgiveness of our wrongdoing. No longer should we war against other tribes. We must stop taking heads. We must learn the ways of love."

But it was easier for Chawnga to preach about love than to find it in his own home. His actions since he had given his name to Jesus were in sharp contrast to the old traditions, which he had been taught all his life to respect. Many of the village elders, including his own father, Buola, were infuriated over this intrusion from the outside world and the disruption of age-old tribal traditions.

When he could not convince his son to renounce his new faith, Buola disinherited him. An outcast from his family, Chawnga at first found it difficult to convince others to follow.

However, one by one, there were other converts. His skill at preaching increased. Soon he was traveling up and down the mountains to proclaim God's truth. Often one of his friends, Hlunte, would go with him. Another convert, Thangnura, discovered that he had a gift for music and composed deeply meaningful songs around Scripture passages which he had memorized.

The young converts memorized entire books of the Bible. Since none of the tribespeople could read or write, oral communication was the only way they could share the gospel.

As the years passed, Chawnga became known as "the preacher on the mountain." He had married a young tribal girl named Daii and settled in Senvon. Daii was a dedicated believer, as were, by now, *several hundred* other Hmars.

In time Chawnga and Daii started a family. A girl was born first, but later died. Ramlien was the firstborn son. Next, another son was born. They named him Rochunga ("God's highest inheritance"), at the suggestion of his grandfather (Daii's father), who had become a Christian.

Rochunga, nicknamed Ro, had heard his father tell the story of Watkin Roberts so often that it had made an indelible impression in his mind. In the fifteen years since the coming of Mr. Young Man, the tribe had several thousand believers—all without the help of missionaries from the outside world. Influenced only by the indirect training of Watkin Roberts, the original five converts had taken the gospel of Jesus to the 3,000 people in Senvon, as well as to the tribes in the neighboring Phulpui and Vangai areas.

When Ro was almost ten years old, he and his family heard the bad news about Mr. Young Man. Roberts had gone to America and had been successful in raising financial and prayer support for his work from churches in Pennsylvania, Ohio, and Illinois. He had even hired an American to look after the work at the American headquarters. However, his new associate had other plans. He booked passage to India and once on the mission field, "fired" Roberts and claimed executive leadership for himself.

The American visited the native Christian leaders where Watkin Roberts had been working. "From now on," he ordered, "you will be working for me. *I* am your new chief. You will be loyal to *me.*"

Chawnga and the others were unanimous in their response. "No, we are loyal to Jesus," Chawnga told the American via the interpreter. "We know Mr. Young Man. We do not know you. Mr. Young Man was not our chief. He was our brother, an equal."

"But you are not qualified to preach."

"Mr. Young Man has taught us. God's Spirit makes his words clear. We have already many Christians in our tribe."

"But you're not qualified," the American repeated.

Chawnga shrugged. "Our loyalty is to God and our brother, Mr. Young Man."

Incensed, the American went to another missionary organization for advice. The leaders were sympathetic. They, too, had heard of the unaccredited missionary from Wales who had "gone native" in the hills of Manipur.

Together the established mission leaders went to the British authorities, who in turn referred the matter to their political agent, a tough-minded man named Gimson.

An edict went out to the hill tribes:

Unless you cooperate with the Western missionaries, your practice of the Christian religion will be suspended. We cannot place the Christian gospel in the hands of ignorant men. Unless you cooperate with the missionaries, your church leaders will be arrested and your churches disbanded.

At the Hmar village, Chawnga considered the edict. Already the seeds of disruption were taking their toll. The church was being split. Most, like Chawnga, continued in their goal of converting Hmars to Christianity, still under the leadership of Watkin Roberts. But the American had convinced some of the church elders and there was a split. Some believers started rival groups in the same villages. Where the Christians had established a village school, now the American's group had a school. The people were confused: which school or church should they attend?

Soon the word went out across the hills. The Christians who were part of Roberts' Mission were "outlaws," forbidden by the British to practice their religion, even to have schools or churches in the state of Manipur.

The British took the edict further than the Western mission leaders had asked. Actually, they only wanted Watkin Roberts discredited and eliminated so they could evangelize the area according to traditional colonial methods. Political agent Gimson, however, was determined to teach the tribals a lesson.

He ordered the Hmar and Lushai Christians from the newly formed Burma Pioneer Mission organization arrested and brought before him. At these unorthodox trials, the believers were ordered to drop their allegiance to Roberts

and cooperate with the Western missionaries. "Coopera-
tion" meaning submitting to their leadership and authority.
Most of the tribals refused. The result was either a jail
sentence, public beating, or both.

One day, runners excitedly approached Chawnga's village.

"Soldiers are coming! Soldiers on horseback!" they cried.

Such visits were seldom social in nature. The natives
scurried to their houses, seeking sanctuary behind the thin
bamboo walls.

"Chawnga! Political agent Gimson wants to talk with you!"
Lieutenant Thanga barked. He was a stern Lushai warrior,
who wore the bush jacket and wide-brimmed cavalry hat of
the British pony soldiers.

Chawnga felt his wife's hands dig into his arm. He placed
his hand on her shoulder to reassure her. "God gives me
peace for this," he whispered to his wife. He nodded to
Ramlien and young Rochunga, who glared at the soldiers.
"My sons, you help your mother until I return."

"Yes, father," the boys replied in obedient unison.

A soldier tied Chawnga's hands and led him to the horses.
The villagers watched with growing anger. Perhaps it was
time to stand up to the outsiders.

"You steal our dignity!" cried a Hmar youth.

"Leave us alone!" yelled another.

"Give back Chawnga. He does no harm to you."

The voices encouraged one another. By now the small
crowd numbered close to 100.

Several young men had grabbed spears and were push-
ing toward the soldiers. There were only a half-dozen soldiers, and the Hmars could easily overpower them.

Lieutenant Thanga sensed trouble. He spurred his horse
and commanded his soldiers to follow. Chawnga was jerked
by the rope fastened to a saddle horn. He half ran, half
stumbled to keep up.

The crowd charged after them. Suddenly a rifle shot
drowned out their cries and silenced them.

"Stop right there," Lieutenant Thanga ordered, "or I will
have my men open fire."

"Please do as he says," Chawnga pleaded. "Go back to
your houses and pray."

Murmuring, the crowd reluctantly backed off.

Chawnga was placed astride a horse with his hands still
tied in front of him. With rifles lowered and pointing toward
the villagers, the soldiers moved away slowly. When they
were safely away from the village, they resumed a military
column formation and galloped toward the British agent's
compound.

The compound was more like a mansion to Chawnga,
who had never seen how the white people lived. Servants
scurried about everywhere. The walls were made of stone
and wood, not bamboo. And the white marble floors glowed
with the reflected radiance of the afternoon sun.

Gimson was not wearing a British uniform. His linen suit
was tailored in a military style, however. The British agent
had another man with him. Lieutenant Thanga translated for
the agent and Chawnga.

"British agent Gimson and the missionary Mr. Abernathy
want to question you, Chawnga."

Gimson's words were clipped and precise. "You may
address this native, Reverend Abernathy."

"Yes, sir, thanks," said the American.

Turning to the lieutenant, he said, "Please translate for
me. Ask this man who gave him permission to preach the
gospel to his tribe. Ask him by what authority he preaches."

While the Lushai translated, Chawnga listened. Then he
answered. When he finished speaking, the American seemed
impatient.

"What did he say?" Abernathy asked.

"Chawnga says, 'In the year of flowering bamboo, a white
missionary we call "Mr. Young Man" came to the Hmar
people.'"

"He must be talking about Roberts. But he's not a *credentialed* missionary."

"Yes." Lieutenant Thanga continued his translation. "'This man is missionary. He live in Hmar village, wear Hmar tribal clothes, eat Hmar food, and tell Hmar people of Creator God and his Son, Jesus.'"

"Yes," Abernathy's voice hardened. "I heard that Roberts had 'gone native,' defying orders, and had sneaked into the hills without a permit. We had to expel him from his own missionary organization."

Abernathy seethed in anger for a moment, then stiffened to regain his composure. "Tell this good man," he said to the Lushai, "that we're here to take the place of this uh—missionary Roberts. We will build a church for the Hmar Christians."

Lieutenant Thanga translated and Chawnga replied; then the soldier turned back to Abernathy. "Chawnga say that to the Hmar people no one can take the place of missionary Roberts. He say also that Hmars already have built not one church, but many. He say, 'Please, the greatest blessing you can bestow on Hmar people is to let them alone.'"

Gimson intervened at this point. He said sharply, "Now you listen to me! You and your people shall accept the help offered by Reverend Abernathy and his people. Translate!" he ordered the soldier.

When Chawnga heard the agent's words, his face showed no emotion.

"Well?" Gimson asked impatiently.

Chawnga's reply was brief. "Chawnga will accept help only from God and his Spirit."

"Enough of this impertinence! Take him to the courtyard for punishment!" yelled Gimson.

Lieutenant Thanga reluctantly led Chawnga away.

In the courtyard they tied the Hmar preacher to a post. His shirt was torn off, and a soldier approached to administer the beating. Reverend Abernathy and Gimson stood by the wall as witnesses.

"Is it really necessary to go this far?" Abernathy asked Gimson.

"The·law is the law. We must make an example here."

The beating would be done with a solid cane stick. It was not like bamboo, which is hollow. It was a thick rod which would not bend or break. Chawnga knew of other Hmar believers who had preferred to be punished rather than to submit. Some had broken ribs. Two men, Thangnura and Kappu, had been so badly beaten that their internal organs were severely bruised. It was two days before they could even pass urine.

Chawnga braced for the beating. The cane came down upon his back unmercifully and relentlessly. The blows struck his muscular back; nerve endings caught the full pain as the skin welted and lacerated. A shock wave of pain smashed through the rib cage and jolted his insides.

Chawnga wanted to scream out in pain, but instead clenched his jaw. He forced his mind to concentrate on the sufferings of Jesus and the beatings of the Apostle Paul. He would endure pain and suffering as they had, and God would give him the strength and grace to endure.

After a while it ended. A soldier splashed a bucket of water on Chawnga's back to wash away the blood. To the sensitive and broken skin, the water felt like another blow from the cane.

Someone cut the rope tying his hands to the post, and the Hmar preacher sagged to the ground. Another soldier picked up Chawnga's torn shirt and without bothering to shake off the dirt threw it over Chawnga's shoulders.

"Let him walk back to his village," Gimson ordered. "It will give him plenty of time to reconsider his position."

It wasn't until several days later that Chawnga stumbled back to Senvon village. No one seemed to notice his return, nor did he call attention to it.

Daii gasped and cried when she saw her husband pull himself up the steps of their house.

The two boys ran to help their father.

"Father!" cried Ro, who had now turned ten.

Chawnga sat in front of the *tap* (hearth), made of hard-packed clay framed by wooden braces. All the cooking was done here. He asked for some rice and tea, having had nothing to eat since his arrest.

Daii rushed to fix her husband something to eat. Ramlien grabbed a bamboo tube filled with water and offered his father a drink. Ro looked at the dried blood which had oozed through the torn and dirty shirt. He offered to help his father take off the shirt so they could wash his wounds and apply bear grease and herbs to the back. But the shirt had been in place too long. As he tried to take it off, Chawnga cried out. The cuts and lacerations had stopped bleeding, but the shirt had become part of the scabs. When the shirt was removed, all the wounds reopened with a sharp and painful reminder of the beating.

The wounds were washed and tenderly treated with the medicinal ointments of the tribe. Then Chawnga went to bed, his aching, throbbing body finally able to rest.

Young Ro watched his father sleep fitfully. He had a strange feeling in his stomach as though he, too, had been beaten. For both father and son, life would never again be the same.

Chawnga and young Ro looking toward the horizon, which Chawnga compares to God's love—always there, always waiting. Scene from the film *Beyond the Next Mountain*

FOUR
NEW HORIZONS

Ro had grown up in the jungles with all the experiences common to the small Hmar boys. He had played among the tombstonelike slabs of rocks where his grandfather, Buola, had sacrificed cows and chickens to please the spirits. Some had even sacrificed men and women to appease *Khawhri* (evil spirit).

Chawnga had told his sons about *Khawhri*, as well as other spirits—*Khawchawn, Khuovang, Zasam, Phung,* and *Lasi.* But the Hmars no longer feared the roving spirits. Nearly all in the village were Christians, who worshiped the Creator God and his Son, Jesus.

"The forest is our home," Ro's father had once told him, pointing out the tangle of vines hanging from great trees which blocked out the sun. The boy knew his father was about to tell him a story, either about their past and the Hmar history or about a principle for living as a Christian. Ro enjoyed these stories and the companionship of his father.

Chawnga continued, "The forest is also the home of many wild animals."

Ro nodded. "This morning I saw a big track in the river's mud."

"The Royal Bengal tiger lives in our woods," Chawnga

explained. "You must learn quickly that a tiger talks with his tail."

Ro already knew that. He was glad to repeat what his father had told him before. "If he does not put his tail all the way under his legs, then you know he is interested in you for food," he said. "A tiger can kill a cow with one blow, and he can eat you up very fast."

"Very good, my son," Chawnga smiled. "A tiger will not eat you if you know his plan."

Ro recalled chasing a tiger once. The Hmars had bamboo huts about six feet off the ground to keep the jungle dampness from penetrating the split-bamboo flooring. The space below the house was used as a corral for goats, pigs, chickens, and other livestock. One night, a desperate tiger boldly entered the corral and carried off a large pig. The other livestock set up a commotion that awakened nearly the entire village. Grabbing a bamboo stick, Ro thrust it into the dying embers of a fire until flames blossomed at the end. Then he ran with the other Hmars into the night. The tiger was so strong he ran a half mile before dropping his two-hundred-pound body to rest. When the Hmars noticed that, they followed the weary tiger with such commotion and waving of torches that the big cat finally abandoned his kill. The scene of the tiger dragging a large pig for half a mile registered properly in Ro's memory.

Herds of wild elephants also passed near the village. If they got angry, the large beasts sometimes ran right through the village.

One day Ro's father took him to watch a herd of elephants feeding near the river. Chawnga explained, "My son, an elephant's tail also speaks to us. Can you tell me what it says?"

"Yes, Father," Ro said. "If an elephant's tail is up, you should be gone. An elephant can squash a man before he can run."

Chawnga nodded. "And what can you tell me about the monkeys in our forest?"

"Monkeys are like noisy children. They like to play and laugh. Sometimes I climb a tree and try to swing through the air like the monkeys. But they always go away and I have to come down to the ground and play with the other children," Ro said.

"You should know also that a monkey is the watchdog of the forest. He warns of danger if we listen carefully," Chawnga instructed.

"My father," Ro finally asked, "why did they beat you?"

"They do not know our ways," Chawnga answered simply. "They think the Hmar people are like animals in the forest."

"If only Mr. Young Man would come back. He would tell us what to do," the boy said.

"He is not coming back, boy. Never. He has been sent away from India forever." Chawnga had not told anyone of this news.

"Gone?" Ro asked incredulously. "But why?"

His father did not answer directly, but Ro knew his words were not intended to be wasted. "Mr. Young Man will not come back, my son. If we are to be free, someone who knows our ways must help us. Our help must come from our own tribe."

Ro learned much from his father. There were other influences in his life, however.

Often when his father was away preaching, Ro would run with other boys in the village. Some were older, almost old enough to move to the *buonzawl.*

Ro fished and hunted with them. Sometimes they would go into the forest to catch wild pheasants. They would set either snares baited with grains of rice, or cagelike traps made of sharpened bamboo. Sometimes they would hunt with bows or slings. When there were no pheasants, the boys sometimes caught large white jungle rats, prized as much as chickens for eating.

One day the boys caught a large rat and put it in a bamboo cage. "Rochunga," Hmingte said to him, "do you still want to be a member of our band?"

Hmingte's group consisted mostly of younger toughs who had a reputation for pranks and mischief. They often set snares which tripped women going to the stream for water. Sometimes they would steal firewood from smaller boys and claim it as their own.

Ro knew there was an initiation to join the gang, but he still wanted to be a part of the group.

"What must I do?" Ro asked.

"You must perform an act of bravery," Hmingte grinned. "Are you willing?"

Ro nodded.

"Then take the rat in that cage and skin it alive—with your own teeth!"

At first Ro thought he was joking. But he saw he was not.

"I must test your loyalty and obedience," Hmingte said. "If you do not do this, we will all beat you!"

Reluctantly, Ro chased the rodent to the corner of the bamboo cage and grabbed it. His small hand held the jaws shut and kept the rat's razorlike teeth in check, but the sharp claws swiped at him.

Ro swallowed hard and closed his eyes as his teeth bit into the furry neck of the rodent. Waves of nausea swept over him, but he continued. The squealing rodent was finally put out of its misery when the grisly task was done.

His loyalty and obedience were now unquestioned. In fact, it wasn't long before the other boys in the gang began looking up to Ro more than to Hmingte as a leader. That infuriated the older boy.

One day, Ro and another boy had climbed a tall slender tree. When they were at the top, Hmingte took his *dao* and began to chop the tree down. Ro and his companion yelled and tried to climb down, but the tree was swaying too much.

"I will chop off the legs of whoever climbs down!" Hmingte threatened.

Terrified, the two boys could do nothing but hang on. Finally there was a loud cracking sound as the tree broke and began to topple. Both boys hit the ground with such force that neither got up right away. At last Ro shook his head in a daze, but otherwise he was all right. His companion, however, lay very still on the jungle floor.

"Tana!" Ro cried out. "He's dead! You've killed him!"

Hmingte and the others began to run. "Don't tell anyone," Hmingte snarled as he left, "or you will die also!"

Tears began to run down Ro's cheeks. Frightened, he did not know what to do. Then he heard a soft moan.

"Tana! Are you alive?" He dropped down to the motionless figure. Tana moaned again and fluttered his eyelids. In a few minutes he sat up and felt all right. After that experience, Ro lost interest in Hmingte's gang.

The next Sunday evening, as Ro's father, Chawnga, was preaching, Ro felt convicted of his wrongdoing. He sat in the back of the little bamboo church with its thatched roof and listened to his father recite the thirteenth chapter of John's Gospel:

"'Now before the feast of the Passover, when Jesus knew that his hour was come that he should depart out of this world unto the Father, having loved his own which were in the world, he loved them unto the end.'"

The Hmars' rough translation concluded with "He loved them as far as the horizon." The tribal preacher continued, speaking to his people about the greatness of God's love and its extent and depth. He also spoke about man's sinful spurning of God's love.

Though only about ten years old, Ro was drawn by his father's sermon. He saw himself the servant of the gang leader and the slave of sin.

Chawnga's sermon explained salvation in clear terms. Even a boy could not mistake the tug of God's Spirit. Ro walked solemnly to the front of the church when his father extended an invitation to all who wanted to follow Jesus to come forward and say so publicly.

"My father," the boy said quietly, "I believe, and I have asked Jesus to forgive me."

"And so he has," Chawnga told him.

"You have said God has written in his book that he for-gives those who ask him. If it is written, it must be so. God would not lie, would he, my father?"

"No, my son. It is true. It is written in his book," the preacher reassured his son.

"Is it really so? Are you certain he will forgive me?"

"What do you believe?" the father asked.

"I believe in God and that Jesus died for my wrongdoing. I am sorry for my sins, and I want Jesus to forgive me."

"Did you pray and ask him?" Chawnga asked.

"I did, my father. And you have said he will forgive me. But are you certain he will do it?" Ro questioned.

"He has given his word. He will not lie," Chawnga said simply. "It is written in his book."

The next day Chawnga took his son up to the mountain where he always went to pray.

"Have you read God's book, my father?"

"His book is not in the Hmar language, but Lushai. But many Hmars understand."

"I would like to learn how to read God's book," the boy said.

Chawnga weighed his words carefully. "It is not an easy matter, my son. It is necessary that someone make a lan-guage for writing our words. Then someone can interpret God's book in the words of the Hmars. My son, I pray that God will send someone to write the Hmar language and write God's book and give it to all the Hmars."

"You can do it, my father. You are very wise."

"No, my son. I do not have the learning. Some of us can read the Lushai language. But no writing exists in Hmar. It will take much learning," the preacher answered.

"How much learning will it take, my father? Can I get such learning?"

Chawnga looked into Ro's intense eyes. "There is no school in our village," he replied. "You must go to Chu-rachandpur Mission School. It is ninety-six miles to the morning sun."

Young Ro had no idea how far that was, except that it would take a journey of six days and nights to get there. He sighed sadly, "My legs are too short."

Chawnga laughed. "Are they not long enough to reach the ground? God would be with you on such a journey, my son."

"Are you certain, my father?"

"Yes, why do you ask?"

"You said in the Lord's Day sermon that God's love will surround me."

"Yes, his love is as wide as the horizon."

"But I can see the horizon. Over there is the mountain which hides the Barak River. Churachandpur is far beyond that. I cannot see that far. I will lose the love of God if I go to school," the boy reasoned.

Chawnga and the boy walked to the top of the mountain. "God's love is as far as the horizon, my son. But you do not see the horizon."

Father and son stood silently, contemplating the beauty and the danger which were interwoven in both the mountains and jungles. Chawnga raised his right hand while resting his left one on his walking staff. He pointed.

"Across the valley, many days' journey, is the tea plantation of the English. There your grandfather and other Hmar warriors took many heads in battle." The hand moved again, pointing far away. "And can you see at the far end of the valley—there in the clouds—another mountain?"

"Oh, yes, my father! I have seen it many times."

"If you climb to the top of the far mountain, what will you see?"

"I do not know."

"You will see still another mountain. And can you see at the top of the mountain where the sky touches the earth?"

"Yes, sir."

"It is called 'the horizon.'" Chawnga lowered his eyes from that distant point to rest upon his son. "Wherever you journey, my son," he said quietly, "the horizon always stays just in front of you—beyond the next mountain."

Chawnga raised his eyes again. "God's love is like the horizon—always there, waiting for us and leading us on."

Chawnga fell silent, his eyes sweeping over the jungles and the mountains, wondering if his young son could grasp the vastness of God's love and the significance of what he had just told him.

For a long time, Ro was also still, his brown eyes roaming across the expanse, past the jungles waiting at the bottom, up the next hill, down, up. . . . Then he sat down in the thick green grass and gazed thoughtfully once again at the distant peaks. Finally he spoke, "My father, I want to give my name to Jesus. I want to be the one to find learning and make a language for God's book. For this learning I will follow him to the horizon."

FIVE
DANGEROUS JOURNEY

No mother would think lightly of sending her ten-year-old son on a journey alone, traveling ninety-six miles through dangerous jungles. Daii knew that Chawnga and Ro had rehearsed the plan very carefully. The boy would go with angels watching over him. Daii was anxious despite the faith of her husband. She too had faith, but there would be no harm in praying for her boy.

Her prayers were emotional, almost a chant. She prayed all night before the morning the boy was to leave. Daii's prayers were of a practical nature—petitions for the boy's safety and the right companions so that he would not be led into sin. Chawnga prayed with her, asking for God's help in guiding their son to the knowledge necessary for translating God's book into the Hmar tongue.

Ro rose at dawn the next morning and heard the sound of his mother's prayers from the *sawngka*. He ate some rice she had prepared and gathered his few belongings. From his waist belt hung a small pouch containing flint and tinder, a small knife, and some leather thongs to make snares for small game. Also hanging from his belt was a bamboo tube, cut and shaped to serve as a canteen.

Finally he picked up a small bamboo cage for trapping birds or squirrels. Wrapping a *puon* around his waist and throwing a second one over his shoulders, Ro was ready to go.

He embraced his mother, who could not gaze directly into his face. He sensed her anxiety and tried to act brave.

"I will work very hard, my mother," he said smiling. "You will be proud of me. Please do not be afraid. I am not afraid. God goes with me."

Daii held her son tightly for a long moment, then let him go. Her eyes still had not met his, and she closed them. So as to not betray her tears, Daii began to pray once more, but this time her voice was strained. It was almost impossible for her to maintain her composure. Would this be the last time she would ever see her son?

The boy edged slowly down the steps of the porch to where his father was waiting. It was impossible for Ro to know what his father was thinking. His face was expressionless, but his eyes seemed to have the same misty glaze as Daii's. Neither spoke as the two walked toward the morning sun.

A herd of elephants was grazing just beyond the jungle clearing. One beast turned toward father and son. Young Ro tried not to show concern.

His father saw him flinch and placed a hand on his shoulder. "If an elephant chases you," Chawnga began as one of the great animals trumpeted loudly, "run straight ahead. Then, make a sharp turn to the right. Move straight again, and make another right turn. Four times and you will be back on your path."

"But that rogue is big. His trunk will smash me on a tree!"

Chawnga shook his head. "All elephants are left-handed. They cannot turn quickly to the right. They always fall to the ground when they try to turn to the right. They can turn only left. It takes an elephant a long time to get up, my son, and you will be far away!"

Chawnga paused and then added, "Satan is like a rogue elephant. He is left-handed, too. In the outside world, Satan will try to lead you into sin. When evil tempts you, tell Jesus about it, and he will tumble Satan on his back!"

"Will I know, my father, when I am tempted?"

"You will know," his father answered softly.

The two were long past the elephants now. Chawnga pointed to the path leading into the jungle. He had already told Ro he could reach Churachandpur by following the path by the river. He had seen to it that Ro could repeat the directions easily before letting him go. Chawnga's voice dropped to a whisper as he fell to his knees and held his son close. He said simply, "God keep you!"

They clung together for a long time. Ten-year-old Ro and his father both knew well the dangers to which Ro was exposing himself. But the rewards were greater than the dangers, and Chawnga had prayed for many weeks, committing his son to the care of him who loves all people everywhere.

Ro started off. The jungle sounds—sometimes strange, sometimes threatening—seemed to leap out, terrifying him. Ro suddenly whirled and raced back to the safety of his father's strong arms. There was another long, silent hug—a final strengthening of father and son for the terrible separation and the great goal which separated them.

Again, Ro started for the jungle. He thought, *I cannot shame my father by looking back a second time.* He thought about his father carefully explaining the dangers in the same matter-of-fact way he had taught Ro to fish: "Watch the path for bears. Pythons will hang in the trees, so also watch above you. Remember that the great snake is afraid of the blue pheasant, whose sharp beak will break his crown."

Tribal lore provided much sage advice. For some reason, the python had a marking on its crown which resembled a nut which the blue pheasant craved. The spot on the snake's head was vulnerable to the sharp beak, and the birds, according to the Hmars, could kill a great python that way. Chawnga had taught Ro how to make the sound of the blue pheasant and snap a twig to sound like a nut being cracked.

So, the Hmar boy walked in the jungle, moving instinctively toward the horizon and the Churachandpur Mission School. Again the jungle sounds assaulted the lone, barefooted boy as he made his way through the countless dangers which lurked around him.

Ro had traveled about three hours when he spied a python on an overhead branch. His heart pounded at the sight. Once he had seen a twenty-five-foot snake swallow a goat. Another time, he had heard of a young calf engulfed by the reptile's powerful, unhinged jaws. It was a thought to make Ro shiver, for he knew that other pythons still lay ahead. He might not always see them.

"When you pass below," his father had warned Ro, "they can drop without a sound and wrap around you. They squeeze away your life with their muscles in order to swallow you whole!"

Ro prayed. "Oh, Lord! What learning can be mine in a great snake's belly?"

The boy remembered what his father had taught him: "The sound of a nut being cracked is enough to send a python slithering to safety." Ro pressed a twig between his fingers until it snapped softly. It sounded, he hoped, like a blue pheasant cracking a nut. Overhead, the python must have thought the same thing, or so it seemed, for the ugly creature crawled away, up into the trees. Ro hurried safely underneath the branch and moved on.

He came to the Barak River and scouted the banks for crocodiles. The river was high and swift, but like all Hmar boys, Ro was a good swimmer. Yet he was also small and had no weight to pit against the rushing current. Ro cut a ten-foot length of hollow bamboo and made a pack out of his *puon* to help him cross the torrent. Ro chose the spot he wanted on the opposite shore, then walked upstream a considerable distance until he judged that the amount of his drift in the mighty current would be about right. Then he shoved off.

The bamboo log kept his face above water, but the current spun him around. He almost lost his belongings twice. The log slipped from his grasp and spun in the slippery water. His small fingers grabbed and missed as the log was carried away. Ro swam toward it in an effort to catch it. He lunged and caught it, struggling back onto it. Kicking his way across, he landed a considerable distance from where he wanted, but made it back to the trail without too much difficulty.

I wonder, Ro thought that night, *how did my mother know I would be too frightened to hunt this first day of my trip to the outside world?*

Ro took out a folded-up green leaf that Daii had put in his pouch. Wrapped inside the leaf was a big helping of cooked rice. When he had eaten, he tried to ignore the mysterious jungle sounds and spread one *puon* for a bed. He struck flint against the side of his small metal flintbox until flying sparks ignited the dry, gray moss he'd gathered from the sheltered roots of trees. He built up the fire and laid dry wood nearby to keep the flames alive through the night. Then he lay down, listening to the crickets and the many notes of the different tree frogs. He was also certain that he had heard the sudden stealthy sounds of some big, unseen animal watching him. But it kept its distance from the boy and his fire.

His father's words came back to Ro: "All the animals in the forest are created by God. He gave each its ways."

But Ro's question, asked silently in the fearful night, was, *God, will you favor me over the night creatures that sound so hungry?*

A tiger's guttural snarl answered Ro. The boy stiffened, instinctively wanting to pull the second *puon* over his head. But his training from earliest childhood had been, "Never cover your head when a tiger is near. For some reason we Hmars do not know, the tiger will not attack a sleeping man with his head uncovered. But if you cover your head, the tiger will attack."

Ro had heard of such attacks. In the night, Ro listened,

lying still and trying to ignore the mosquitoes which hummed about his eyes, nose, mouth, and ears. After a long time, apparently frustrated by the fire, the tiger quit circling and growling. The jungle never quite became still, but the night sounds became more commonplace, so Ro slept.

Morning arrived in the jungle, and Ro was awakened by the squeals of monkeys. He knew that today he would come to the big lake with more mountains beyond. Ro had set his snares the night before and caught a large pale squirrel. He quickly killed and roasted the rodent over the coals of his fire.

All day Ro traveled on, scooping water from streams to refill his bamboo canteen, using his *puon* against the sun in place of an umbrella, and eating berries and wild fruit when he was hungry.

The boy kept a sharp eye out for unfriendly neighboring tribes. Chawnga had warned him that in times past, some had captured the weak or those traveling alone and kept them as slaves. These "child lifters" were from tribes where the gospel had not yet penetrated. Some still practiced head hunting.

Ro passed through one stretch of jungle and began to climb up the steep hill which graduated into another immense mountain. The ascent was steep, but at least he was out of the jungle for a while and could walk though the tall grass. As he started down a small incline before the next climb, he saw a small bear cub on the trail. Instinctively, Ro reached down and picked up the animal.

It let out a squeal. An angry roar rumbled from the nearby brush. Immediately, a female bear rushed toward Ro. All he saw was an immense jaw and hideous teeth. He dropped the cub and sprinted down the hill some distance before daring to look back.

Again Chawnga's words came back to the boy: "If a bear chases you, do not run uphill. It will catch you. Run downhill. A bear has two legs in back which are longer than his front legs. It cannot run fast downhill without falling." When he did look back, Ro saw the mother tenderly caressing the cub with her tongue and occasionally looking toward Ro, threatening him with horrible growls.

He slept the second night, trying to ignore the dangers which lurked just beyond the protective circle of his fire. He thought about his father and knew that Chawnga was going often to the mountaintops, his face uplifted in prayer or his head on his knees. As he often did, Chawnga would no doubt forget about the time and be in prayer a long time. When night would come, he would simply wrap his red, black, and yellow *puon* over his shoulders and offer prayers for his son's safety.

The next morning, Ro picked up an unwanted traveling companion. A *keipui* (huge Royal Bengal tiger), splendidly striped in orange and black, started walking alongside the jungle path, but some distance ahead of the boy. The big cat rumbled deep in his massive chest. His huge head and yellow eyes turned often toward the small brown boy who tried not to hurry or show fright.

"Oh, Lord!" Ro's prayer was lost in the big cat's grumbling growl. "Oh, Lord!" The boy was too frightened to say more, but he remembered that God would know his thoughts, which were quite fearful at the moment.

For several hours the tiger kept pace beside Ro, but never moved in closer. Sometimes the cat would vanish briefly in the dense undergrowth, but it always reappeared, accompanied by the unmistakable rumbling growl which could be heard for great distances, warning all in their path of clear danger.

Suddenly Ro saw the tiger in a different light. "Oh, Lord! Thank you! You have sent the tiger to *protect me* from the headhunters and the wild creatures who might eat me! None of them wants to meet up with that tiger!"

Ro lost his "guide" at another river, but now he was into the open ground again and the dangers were less. He was convinced more than ever that God had provided the tiger as his escort to bring him safely through the most dangerous part of his journey. He climbed another mountain, paused at the top to see that yet another jungle and range lay between him and the horizon. Then the boy moved on again.

For the third night, Ro camped. He thought as he stared into his lonely fire, *I do not know the meaning of ninety-six miles. It must be far because after three days and nights in the jungle, I am just halfway.*

In the morning, Ro pushed on toward the horizon, remembering that God's love went even beyond that and that somewhere in between was a village school. He climbed a banyan tree to try to catch sight of the school. The banyan, a gigantic tree with a complex root system above ground, had thick branches with lower ropelike vines to the ground. The living braces which supported the thick limbs could grow until that one tree might eventually cover several acres. But as big as the tree was, Ro could not see the school from his vantage point.

He moved on, then took shelter from a storm under some broad-leafed plants. His second *puon* helped keep off the torrents of rain which poured from the angry sky. But the storm soon passed, and Ro resumed his journey.

Ro walked along the now muddy trail. His feet were bruised and cut from numerous sharp stones and thorns.

Climbing down a slippery mud bank, the boy lost his balance and fell nearly eight feet. He landed on the edge of his foot and sprained his left ankle. For a long while he sat massaging the painful ankle, then hobbled to a cane plant nearby. With his knife, he whittled it into a crude walking staff and leaned on it heavily as he continued his journey. His foot soon grew tired and swollen.

Later that day, he stopped by a cold rushing stream to soak his sore foot. The cool water eased the pain and tempted him to stay there for the night. However, the rain had raised the level of the stream considerably. With the rainwater running off the mountain, the whole area could be flooded by morning. The current was already racing.

Ro studied the situation carefully. The river was too dangerous to swim across. He would be swept downstream and over the falls, for sure. The waterfall was nearly sixty feet high. The boy walked to where the water thundered over the edge. Debris had collected on the rocks just above the falls. Carefully, the boy held his belongings high and eased his way onto one of the rocks.

He moved cautiously onto a log which shifted slightly but held his weight. He edged along its length and jumped onto another rock, then hopped across two more boulders to safety on the other side of the stream. Ro slowly let out his breath, knowing that he would sleep well that night.

The next day was fairly uneventful. His foot still bothered him, but did not interfere with his schedule.

The boy had been alone five nights on the trail, and was well into the afternoon of the sixth day when he heard a different sound. It was not of the jungle.

Ro hurried forward through the tall cane, which was taller than he was. At last he stepped into a clearing. He saw fences unlike the bamboo ones his tribesmen put up around their livestock. This fence was made of cut boards. Next he saw several small, rusted buildings of corrugated iron sheeting.

Ro walked forward uncertainly, his legs sore and his feet swollen, scratched, and bruised. He had walked ninety-six miles closer to the morning sun—six days closer to the horizon.

The laughter of children at play told Ro that he had reached his first goal. Ro had arrived for school in Churachandpur.

SIX
STUDENT, RUNNER, TRADERMAN, WHO?

The next four years would pass quickly for young Ro. His sprained ankle and swollen, cut feet would be long forgotten.

Chawnga had made arrangements for Ro to live with a young medic and his family from the mission clinic at Churachandpur. The cost for room and board would be three rupees per month (about forty-five cents) plus whatever work the ten-year-old could handle. Ro seemed capable of caring for dairy cows, his providers decided, so each morning before sunrise, Ro would get up and milk thirty-five cows. These Indian cows were "dry," producing relatively little milk; even so, the chore took Ro almost three hours to complete! Then, before breakfast, he would herd them to their grazing pastures. After school, he'd drive the cows back, feed and water them, and then milk all thirty-five again in the evening, a task which went quickly since the cows had very little milk by that time. Of course, Ro was also expected to help with the other chores, such as weeding the garden and cleaning the house.

Ro was envious of the other students who lived in a dorm and played during their free time. Because of his many chores, Ro had no time to play and little time for study. What free time he had was spent studying.

Often, because of the example of his evangelist father, Ro would go out to nearby villages and witness with other students. Most of these tribes were non-Christian, so their reception ranged from cool to hostile. Once, as president of the school's Christian Endeavor group, Ro took several students to Teisieng village six miles from the school. When he tried to talk about Jesus to three men around a fire, one of them reached for his *dao* and cursed him. Ro ran, but another man called after him. As it turned out, the second man wanted to hear the gospel message and later "gave his name to Jesus."

To complicate matters at school, each teacher taught a different subject in his own native tongue. That meant that Ro had to learn *five* different languages before even learning any of his lessons.

Despite the difficulties, Ro was determined to learn. The four years spent at Churachandpur gave Ro an education some students took six years to acquire. By this time Ro had become so proficient that the school appointed him as a teacher for the younger children in the Sunday school. He enjoyed this new role; he also looked forward to getting a better education in the mission high school.

After graduation, Ro went home for the summer and helped his family with the planting and weeding of their small *jhum*. The men often worked on making or repairing tools while the women spun and dyed the cotton they had grown. Later they would weave the cotton into shirt fabric, *puons*, or other material.

By fall the rains had stopped. Ro had planned to apply to the Jorhat Christian High School. However, stories reached the Hmar villages of a great noise "that came from the sky." Workers who were working in the *jhums* when the noise passed said it "covered" them. The outside world had found the Hmars. The noise was the sound of Allied bombers on their way to attack Japanese troop columns marching from Burma into India.

India had long been under English domination. The East India Company had grown powerful in the subcontinent. Political power was vested in the British crown for the next century. When World War II started, India was still a part of the British colonial empire. When the Japanese and Germans declared war on the Allies (which included the United States and Britain), naturally India was involved. The Japanese invasion of the British colonial nation seemed logical and inevitable.

The Hmars reflected on the strange situation in which they had found themselves. The Japanese were considered "the terribles." From a far country in the outside world, they had marched with big guns and frightening machines across the border of Burma into India. The *Raj* told Chawnga, "There is a mad chief called 'Hitler.' He plans to kill every race, and Japanese tribe have joined with him."

The Japanese soon came to many Hmar villages and marched through, pulling small artillery pieces with work elephants confiscated from the Burmese. The people panicked in the border villages as the war surged back and forth. The Japanese invaded, and the Allied Forces roared against them with their jeeps and troops.

History books wouldn't accurately record the behavior of the victorious British and Indian soldiers. They would take not only the Hmars' chickens, pigs, goats, and sheep, but also their young women—whenever they wanted. The Japanese, on the other hand, took nothing from the tribals without offering payment; they respected their women. It made young Ro wonder who the real enemy was.

Ro's patriotism caused him to put aside his ambition to translate the Bible into Hmar. Filled with loyal fervor, Ro, now fourteen, volunteered to serve with the soldiers of the Raj. Five-foot, two-inch Ro barely passed the minimum height requirement to serve in the Raj's army. This unit was a type of British military control force similar to the foreign legion. But no matter how he sucked in his breath and swelled his chest, Ro could not meet the minimum chest-size requirements.

Ro was keenly disappointed. He reasoned, *I am educated. I am even a teacher. I have had to learn Lushai, Paite, Haukip, and Meitei. And I had to learn English. Now the British are drafting soldiers and I want to be in the Army. The Japanese are coming and I cannot go to high school anymore. They are taking my people away and burning their villages. I must do something for my people!*

Perhaps it was a good thing that Ro failed to meet the size requirements of the military. If he had worn a uniform, he would surely have been shot. There were many casualties among his and neighboring tribes. The Hmars and other hill warriors were not sophisticated as were the trained Japanese.

Ro reasoned, *If I volunteer my services as a tribal and wear the tribal* puon, *no Japanese will suspect I speak English. I am not afraid to move through the jungles. I could be a spy for the British.* It was true. The Allied intelligence divisions would be able to use his skills. A special group was being formed by American General Joseph ("Vinegar Joe") Stillwell for just such purposes. The officer in charge of the British sector was stationed in Ro's village.

Ro went to see the officer at night. As he approached the camouflaged tent, the sentry challenged Ro. The young Hmar explained his desire to help his country by being a runner or scout between the American and British camps.

"Pass!" the sentry announced, and Ro went with another soldier to stand outside the officer's tent.

"Lieutenant Broughton, sir!" the soldier said in a loud whisper through the closed tent flaps.

A quiet, but annoyed, English voice came through the tent. "Who is it?"

"Chanderee, sir. I've found a tribal who speaks some English, sir."

"Are you sure he's not armed?" the English officer asked.

"He is unarmed, sir. Shall I have him come in?"

"Very well."

As Ro began to enter the tent, the officer quickly pulled a curtain around the bed, but not before Ro saw the smooth brown back of a pretty native girl, who turned her face to the tent wall. In a flash her nakedness was covered by a drab military blanket. Ro then stepped in all the way and stood while the Britisher held the lantern high and studied the Hmar's face.

Lieutenant Broughton asked, "Do you speak English?"

Ro didn't answer immediately. He looked beyond the officer at the closed drapery, hearing a woman's soft weeping.

The officer demanded, "Do you speak English, I say?"

Ro's eyes focused on the draperies. When the Hmars had marched out of China centuries ago and taken up residence in the Indian jungles, they had never had to lock their doors to protect their women. Highly moral, Ro and his people had now been trying to plan a defense against the sometimes forced, yet often willing, fraternization of the local women and the invading armies. But the Hmars were powerless people and could do nothing. "After all," his friends had told him, "this is what happens in war."

Lieutenant Broughton demanded loudly, "What is your name?"

The Hmar youth suddenly turned his attention to the officer. The white man was in his early twenties, as neat as the wilting humidity of the jungle would permit, and clean-shaven. Ro said quietly, "I am called 'Rochunga.'"

"That's not English!" the officer snapped. "What is your name?"

"Ro-*chun*-ga," Ro repeated. "Son of Chawnga of the Leiri clan."

The officer was still suspicious. Sensing that he needed to establish his credibility, Ro spoke rapidly in his yet imperfect English, "War is making. God save our king! Rochunga is loyal to Raj and want to serve Hmar people and India."

Then he nodded toward the closed drapery. "But I am afraid many of our people have not respect for British soldiers because British soldiers have not respect for Hmar women."

"What's that? What are you trying to say?"

Ro repeated himself and watched the man's face cloud over. The officer's lips tightened and his eyes narrowed, but he chose to ignore the remark.

"Now you listen very carefully," the officer said. "We're in here with strict orders to maintain radio silence. Do you follow me?"

The young Hmar said nothing.

"No, of course, you don't. Then let me put it another way. I need to send messages to the American unit and get messages back from them. It means I need someone who can slip past the Japanese without being detected. Can you find your way about well in these jungles?" Ro nodded yes.

Wearing the Hmar tribal *puon* as a loincloth, Ro began carrying military messages in the hollowed tube of a bamboo canteen. He traveled through the jungles by day, leaped logs, waded streams, and ate cooked rice from a broad leaf as he had years before when he had first walked to school. At night, he slept with a second *puon* pulled over his body, but never over his head. Even with the underbrush filled with Allied and Japanese soldiers, a tiger might still attack a sleeping man who didn't know to keep his head uncovered.

Whenever he stepped out of the jungle into the clearing where Allied troops were stationed, he always heard the click of sentry rifles being cocked and trained on him. Ro would raise his arms to show he was unarmed and an ally.

"Message!" Ro would say quickly and then be conducted by the guards into one of the tents. A white man with a tam and military uniform would read the message, write a reply, and give it back to the youth. Ro would then run back into the jungles with a new message hidden in the bamboo canteen.

Once, Ro jumped a log and scrambled on his hands and knees beneath a low-hanging branch heavy with jungle growth. As he bent to drink from the stream, he heard the unmistakable metallic click of a rifle being cocked. The young Hmar froze. He slowly turned his head toward the sound.

A Japanese soldier squatted a few feet away, his rifle aimed at Ro's heart. Nonchalantly, Ro acted to save his life. Lowering the bamboo canteen to the stream, he quickly scooped up enough water to show that the canteen was for water, but not enough to ruin the message inside. Gesturing to the Japanese soldier, Ro indicated he had just come to the stream to drink and to fill his canteen. If the Japanese had suspected Ro was an Allied runner, he would have shot him at once.

Ro stood up carefully and forced a smile at the sniper. He greeted him in Hmar, *"Chibai! Chibai!"* Then Ro turned his back on the threatening rifle and moved toward the fallen log he'd jumped. The hair stood up on the back of his neck. *Shall I hear the heavy thunder of the rifle before I feel the bullet in my back?* he thought. Ro tried not to think of that until he was safely lost in the shadowed jungle again—after what seemed to be an eternity of anxiety.

Ro arrived at his destination, making his way among the British and Indian soldiers who lounged about their smoky campfires. He announced himself, entered Lieutenant Broughton's tent, and handed over the message. This time the officer was alone.

The officer growled, "It's all wet!" He glanced angrily at Ro, who said nothing. The officer turned back to the message. "But it's legible," he grunted.

In a moment, Lieutenant Broughton leaned back, obviously pleased. "Very good. Jolly well done!"

Ro waited. The lieutenant understood. "Ah, yes! Well,

even soldiers get paid! I'm prepared to give you a little something."

He pulled out a handful of rupees and removed a couple. Counting aloud, he handed them to Ro. "One. Two."

Ro ignored the rupees. He picked up his message tube with his left hand and pointed with his right to a stack of English-made cigarettes on the officer's desk.

The lieutenant shoved the rupees forward. "Look, this money is yours. You've earned it."

Ro pointed again at the cigarettes, ignoring the currency.

Lieutenant Broughton objected. "These are a wartime scarcity. They're as rare as gold. And you know it, don't you?"

Ro didn't move. With a shrug, the officer picked up a pack of cigarettes and reluctantly handed it to Ro.

The young man took the pack and held up one finger; then another finger flicked up.

For a moment, the officer seemed about to refuse, but changed his mind. "One," he said, pointing to the pack in Ro's hand. Broughton handed over the second pack. "Two," he said.

Ro was an instinctively good trader. He thought like a jungle entrepreneur. During his school years at Churachandpur he had augmented his earnings for room and board by trading. He'd take merchandise bought at the mission compound or from the market in town back to the village during his vacation. The villagers were eager to have unusual gifts, medicine, or cigarettes.

Most of the tribals smoked—a custom going back centuries in their tribe. They usually smoked clay pipes. Cigarettes were a novelty many sought after. It was no less true now during wartime when such items were scarce. With packs of cigarettes Ro could trade as a street merchant for other wartime scarcities.

I will go to the Bengalis in Silchar, Ro reasoned. *Those cities are filled with people who have great needs. I have always had a temptation for business. I will also find needles, safety*

*pins, and razor blades. And vitamins. I will knock on doors
and sell the people those scarcities which I can trade for.
Maybe I will even have a street stall like the Bengalis. But first
I must trade my cigarettes for rupees.*

Ro used the cigarettes earned as an Allied spy to build
quite a savings for himself. For some time he served as a
runner for Lieutenant Broughton's troops and the Americans.

Then, just before the end of the war, the intensity of the
battles picked up. On one occasion an American plane was
shot down by Japanese gunners and the crew parachuted
into the jungle. Ro led a rescue party to search for the
downed fliers. He found the injured pilot and escorted him
through the Japanese lines to the Allied camp. If they had
been seen by the Japanese, both would have been shot and
killed instantly.

The Japanese grew more desperate in the waning months
of war. It was no longer safe for a tribal, even in civilian
clothes, to enter the jungle.

Ro decided to plant a *jhum* and wait for the conflict to
end. He worked his land with more intensity and ambition
than any other farmer. It was no surprise, then, that his
small farm yielded twice the grain as his neighbors' farms.
Ro was successful in almost everything he did.

Chawnga also seemed to sense this and asked his son to
accompany him to the mountain where the father went to
pray. "My son, soon the war will end," Chawnga said. "The
Japanese are farther away now, and the Indian troops have
been successful. It will be time for you to go back to school."

"I do not know, my father. . . ." Ro's respect for the tribal
ways made him hesitate to differ with the elder Hmar, but
his honesty would not allow him to deceive his father. "I
have been thinking. I have some education. I am skilled at
trading. In the buying and selling of merchandise, I could
earn many rupees, become rich."

"God is rich enough. He will give us what we need," his
father replied simply. "Perhaps I need to remind you of the
task to which we have dedicated you."

Ro looked at the ground. "My father, I have already studied many years, yet I cannot do the thing you wish. It will take twice as many years as I have already spent. It will take *much* learning. I cannot do it. This schooling is a heavy burden."

"You *must* do it, my son. There is no one else who can do it. Your mother and I have prayed for you since the day God placed you in her womb. It is not just our dream—it is God's plan for you, Rochunga."

"I—I will pray about it, my father. We will see what happens."

Ro had taken his entrance examination during his last year at Churachandpur and now received word that he could enroll at the American Baptist Mission High School at Jorhat, some 400 miles away in Assam. Ro traveled by foot, boat, bus, and third-class railway to the school.

As was the case in elementary school, he had to work for his room and board. His first task, before other students arrived, was to fill in the trenches and foxholes surrounding the school compound. With the end of the war, they were now no longer needed. Ro used a small shovel and a wicker basket to move the earth. It took him two weeks of dawn-to-dusk labor to finish the task. His blisters earned him just enough money to pay for the meals he ate during the same two-week period.

Disappointed that he had no funds for school, he asked for work and was given the much easier job of sweeping and cleaning the dorm for the remainder of his school terms there.

Following the war, Ro was able to juggle his study load with work that paid more money than his job at Jorhat. He was also able to travel back to Silchar, the city with a railroad station. Silchar was alive with activity. American fliers and British troops, along with the many tribal soldiers, came to Silchar for trade and relaxation.

Ro supplemented his high school education with earnings made as a mountain trader. It was in Silchar that he met merchants and skillful traders, such as Prasad. Prasad had ideas, but no money. He convinced Ro to invest his rupees in a trip downriver where a friend had found several dead Army pack mules floating in the water.

"How they died, I do not know," Prasad said. "But I can speculate." The gleam in his eye led Ro to believe there was more to the story than the man was letting on. "Floating alongside the mules were rucksacks, crates, barrels, Army supplies, don't you see? So, my friend loaded them into his boat and brought them to his house. It took him a full-day's work!"

Prasad leaned close to Ro and lowered his voice. "I have seen these goods with my own eyes—canned rations, tinned meat, sugar, malaria pills. People are desperate for malaria pills. But who can afford them?"

"Why do you tell *me*?" Ro asked.

"Because my friend would happily give these things to me. But he must have something for his trouble. He's a poor man. But I have no rupees. You—you, Rochunga, have many rupees."

"But I am saving for school. I will soon finish high school, and I have plans to enter the university."

"Ah, forget school. I have studied at the university and where did it help me? We can be rich, Rochunga. Forget your schooling and come with me," Prasad grinned broadly.

The two rented a sampan (flat-bottomed skiff) and went downriver to meet Prasad's friend. It was exactly as the trader had said. Ro counted out all of his precious rupees. Loading the goods into the boat, Ro and Prasad went back to Silchar and set up a stall.

Prasad and Ro sat on a bamboo mat in a part of the busy city and held up malaria pills and cigarettes to passersby. Soon Indians discovered their stall and began handing rupees to Prasad in exchange for malaria pills.

Silently reaching over, Ro took the rupees from Prasad and put them into a purse. The older Indian shook his head and smiled sadly through his heavily bearded lips. "School, huh? Saving for school? We can do so much with your rupees."

Several weeks passed and the war ended, bringing a new problem—shortages. But these proved to be a blessing to traders with a knowledge of supply-and-demand in the region. As the price of medicine and cigarettes went up, the partnership between Ro and Prasad continued to thrive. Ro now raised three fingers to indicate three rupees for one cigarette. That was as much as he had earned in an entire week as a school boy working in Churachandpur. Now he and Prasad were making 100 times that daily.

One day Prasad said, "The question is, What kind of merchant are you?" He broke off to call to a passing British soldier, "Hello, hello, Tommy boy! Want something? Anything you want is here!"

Prasad swept his hand over the rug on which he and Ro sat, indicating all kinds of souvenirs, novelties, and merchandise. The two partners had a wide variety of other items for sale. Despite their success, however, a tension existed between the Hindu and the Hmar, for Ro was struggling with a deep internal conflict Prasad did not comprehend. Ro was troubled about the unfinished task he'd left and especially about what his father would say when he learned Ro had become a trader and had given up all thoughts of returning to the task of translating the Bible into Hmar.

The weeks slid by, and rupees continued to flow into their hands, but Ro's conscience continued to bother him. He sat silent and brooding, thinking of the long time which had passed since he had dropped out of school and entered his new line of work. His business was thriving. Learning enough to begin translating the Bible meant too many more years of school. Ro sighed, still fighting his internal conflict.

A month or so later Ro looked up as a band playing a lively marching tune went by. He and Prasad were sitting in their stall near the Silchar railroad station. As Ro's eyes swept the large crowd milling about the station, his gaze suddenly stopped on a man dressed in the shirt and *puon* of the Hmar tribe. It was Chawnga! Ro saw him coming, but it was too late for him to do anything.

Prasad called out his wares in various Indian dialects, but switched to English to say, "Smile, Rochunga! Look happy so the people will buy!" Prasad returned to hawking his wares, then again spoke to his partner. "Smile and our sales will go up. Where's your patriotism?"

Chawnga began making his way past the band, which was now marching off in the distance. He walked steadily toward the stall, paying no attention to the monotonous clanging of the railroad crossing bell.

Out of the corner of his eye, Ro could see his father coming closer. Although Chawnga had given no outward sign, Ro knew his father had seen him.

Prasad broke out of his dialect hawking to demand, "What's the matter, Rochunga? Are you ill?"

Ro didn't anwer. Prasad looked up, pleased that someone had stopped at their stall. Chawnga ignored Prasad's hawking and stared silently at his son.

Prasad leaned closer to Ro and whispered, "Is he one of your people?" Ro could only nod.

Chawnga spoke to his son in Hmar. Prasad pursed his lips and raised a questioning eyebrow to Ro, who could not meet his father's eyes.

"What does he want?" Prasad whispered.

Ro translated for his partner, "He says we have many books in our stall."

Chawnga spoke again in Hmar. He knelt and leaned over to be at Ro's eye level.

Ro translated. "He says he wants to buy a book in the Hmar language."

Again, Chawnga spoke, and the young man interpreted. "He wants to buy a Bible in the Hmar language and teach the Hmar people to read."

Having made his point, Chawnga rose and walked away unhappy. Ro followed him, ignoring Prasad, who was unaware of what was going on or of who the Hmar visitor really was.

Chawnga caught up with the slow-moving band before Ro could reach him. The blaring brass drowned out Ro's words. Ro ran after his father and followed him to the other side of the depot and on past the food stalls and market-place. Then Ro caught up with his father. At Ro's request, they entered a roadside tea stall. Chawnga's dark eyes flickered uneasily over the surroundings. He considered tea an unnecessary luxury, and felt out of place.

Father and son sat on the benches in the tea stall. The Bengali proprietor poured them two cups of hot tea from a teapot hanging over an open charcoal fire.

Ro tried to ease the tensions between himself and his father. "How was your journey?" Ro asked.

Chawnga was in no mood for small talk. "It still takes five days. Mountains and rivers have not moved," he said crisply.

Ro changed the subject. "Tea is very good here, Father. I drink often."

"Oh? Like a rich merchant?"

Instead of giving the harsh reply that was on his lips, Ro followed centuries of traditional respect and swallowed before addressing his elder. His voice had an edge of restrained patience. "I have lived with soldiers. I know what money is doing."

Chawnga said nothing, but his eyes spoke volumes. He decided to speak bluntly to his son whom he had traveled so far to find. "All the Hmar people know Chawnga's son is not a student."

Ro defended himself. "I have been to Shillong, my father! I rode a bus to Imphal. I got on and gave the driver a coin, and he took me from Churachandpur to Imphal. The city has many traders. I have learned from them. I know how they do things."

His father said nothing; Ro's explanation for having turned aside from his original mission seemed to fall on unhearing ears. Ro spoke more earnestly. "I do not want to be just one of the poorest! I want to earn a living!"

Chawnga was still unmoved.

Ro tried a new approach. "My father, you told me you work all day in the outside world for one-quarter rupee. Your son has over *100* rupees, and he will have more!"

Chawnga could not help himself. "Does Jesus still have your name?" he barked. It was a full moment before either of them spoke.

Chawnga's persistence to his purpose was clear. "Last Lord's Day," he said, "I preached about the flood in the time of Noah."

Ro looked up at his father, who was now standing up. Chawnga continued, "Sanglien stood up in church. He said he did not believe the story of Noah. He said, 'Water could not cover our mountain!' He laughed and walked away. Others also left with him."

Chawnga's voice slid from a high pitch to a low one as he recounted the painful and embarrassing church episode. "If Sanglien could read the Bible in the Hmar language, he would *know*. . . ."

". . . So much learning will take years, Father!" Ro interrupted. "And a *million* rupees!"

Chawnga's voice was low and compassionate in the tone of a father who understands his son's motivations and obstacles. "It is what I *pray* for you. It is your path to the horizon."

Ro, impatient for his father to finish his tea, shifted uneasily on the bench. His father sensed Ro's restlessness and started to walk away. Ro stood up, paid the bill, and followed Chawnga into the street and toward the river.

On the way Ro tried to restore their relationship by talking about their home village, other shared experiences, and the latest news about family and friends. Finally, they had said everything except the one thing they knew was still foremost in each other's thoughts. However, Ro wasn't anxious to hear what his father was thinking.

Chawnga became silent as they walked. Ro's conscience wrestled with the temptations of business versus the pressing need for time and rupees if he were to return to school and continue preparation for translating the Bible.

Finally, Chawnga, the simple Hmar tribesman of faith, shared his thoughts. "Go to the prime minister. The prime minister will help you."

Ro almost laughed. "The prime minister will not see *me!*"

Chawnga reminded his son of India's newly gained independence. "India is our country now. Tell him the Hmar people are good citizens."

"My father, you have to be big and important to see the prime minister. He will not. . . ."

". . . God will help you," Chawnga interrupted, adding, "I will pray on the mountain."

Ro looked steadily at his father. Chawnga's faith was simple, but Ro suspected it was also a bit naive. After all, he had some education and knew things were generally more complicated than his father allowed. Yet, there was power in the simplicity of his father's faith. He could not deny that.

Ro knew Chawnga would pray, and if his father's faith mattered, God would help Chawnga's son to find some way to see Jawaharlal Nehru, India's first prime minister since independence from British colonial rule had been won. God would also make a way for Ro to resume his education so he could translate the Bible into Hmar.

SEVEN
PURSUING THE DREAM

Ro completed his high school studies at Jorhat and enrolled at St. Paul's College in Calcutta. The school was operated by the London Missionary Society. The war had ended several years earlier and Ro still wavered in his commitment to Chawnga's dream.

He was admitted as a student with a major in economics and political science. Perhaps it was his way of trying to serve two masters.

The Hmar youth had spent half of his life in schools, but now seemed no closer to fulfilling the goal of translating the Bible than before. He finally committed himself to his father's plan. A second year at St. Paul's would hinge on getting a scholarship to the university. The first year of college had taken all his money. If God wanted Ro to continue at the college, God would have to intervene. Ro knew his father also understood this and would be praying on the mountain on his behalf.

Ro wrote in English to the prime minister in New Delhi:

I am a native, born in tribal territory of tribal
parents. I have applied to government for scholarship
available to backward classes and tribal peoples. Since
I am tribal, I meet the qualification for scholarship.

*Yet, when I applied, a letter came back to me to say
I do not qualify because my people, the Hmars, are
not on the nation's census list.*

To his surprise, someone from the prime minister's office
answered his letter. Nehru didn't know of the Hmars, but
was familiar with the Khasis, Nagas, and their neighbors.
"The Hmars will certainly be included in the next census,"
the aide wrote Ro. And, the letter concluded, the scholarship would be granted. Ro and Chawnga were elated.

It was a partial scholarship, which meant Ro had to continue his trading enterprises. However, he was able to earn
enough for room and board by working only on weekends
or holidays to pay expenses. Even at that he had more than
enough study time left.

Ro's biggest difficulty at college was his struggle with
English. He had learned the language from tribal teachers
and soldiers. The sentence structure, syntax, and grammar
weren't as precise as they would have been had he learned
the language in a proper academic setting.

English was so different from his mother tongue. The
Hmar language has no masculine or feminine pronouns,
and the noun object always comes before the predicate. He
kept catching himself saying, "Rice, did you eat it?" instead
of "Did you eat your rice?" He would ask a fellow student,
"Who is that man? I do not know her."

Ro tried to practice English. He memorized words from
the dictionary, struggling until his brain ached from trying
to pronounce the words. He knew it was his most trouble-
some subject. As a student at Jorhat, he had memorized the
English *Book of Common Prayer* and *A Book of Prayers for
the Armed Forces* in an attempt to improve his English.
These had helped, but now he was having trouble again.

Unlike Western school customs, a student in India who
failed a single course had to repeat the *entire* school year.
Ro scored honor roll grades in all other subjects, but failed
an elective English course. He felt even worse when he

learned he had failed that subject by only one point.

He wept bitterly over the bad news. "Do you hate me, God?" he cried out in a prayer of frustration. "My entire future has faded. Even the government scholarship is gone!"

Reluctantly Ro traveled back to the hills of Manipur to tell his parents.

"You must go back to Calcutta and try again," Chawnga said.

"But I cannot," Ro complained. "There will be no scholarship."

His mother looked at him with loving reassurance. "It is the right thing to do. Your father and I have prayed a long time for this. It is the path God wants." Daii put her hand on her son's shoulder.

"I will have a *jhum* this year," she said. "I will plant it and grow chilis, ginger, and rice. We will not have to buy rice. Then we can send you all of your father's salary. My hands will take the hoe, and I will help until you receive your degree!"

Ro felt a catch in his throat; tears welled up in his eyes. With his parents showing such sacrifice and love, how could he do anything less than return to Calcutta?

In Calcutta, he pointed out to school administrators that the English course he failed had been an *elective*. Thus the loss of his scholarship seemed unwarranted. The principal looked at Ro's grades and outstanding records and decided that although Ro would still have to repeat the entire year of courses, he strongly recommended that the government scholarship committee give Ro the scholarship.

Grateful that his mother would not have to work so hard and plant a *jhum*, Ro determined to put everything he had into his studies. He was still concerned about English, however. During devotions, his prayers were always the same, "Lord, help me to learn this most difficult language."

A few days later, a package arrived for him with no return address. Inside was a beautiful leather-bound reference Bible with the fly-leaf inscription: "From a friend in America who loves the Lord and the people of India."

Ro read the entire gift Bible almost nonstop. Then he re-read it. A third time he read from Genesis to Revelation. He would often read the English passages aloud for practice. During that year not only did his English improve, but so did his spiritual understanding.

Ro also attended weekly *Youth for Christ* rallies in Calcutta. The director, Dick Riley, found Ro to be an eager and faithful Christian worker.

Ro now worked only occasionally as an agent for mountain traders and earned several hundred rupees each time. It was more than enough money to meet his needs. Ro had to constantly battle the temptation to leave college and go full-time into business. Helping with the YFC programs took his mind off his temptation.

In addition to helping Dick Riley, Ro also attended the famous William Carey Baptist Church in Calcutta, which had been named for the great missionary who had translated the Bible for believers in India. Ro used William Carey as a role model when he faced the temptation to abandon his goal of translating the Bible for his people.

It was at this time that he indirectly encountered two men who were to influence him profoundly in years to come. The first was Dr. Alan Montforce, who had come to India as an Anglican missionary. His liberal theological doctrines and philosophy were foreign to Ro, but Ro respected Dr. Montforce because of the love he had shown to the Indian people. Dr. Montforce, an admirer of Mahatma Gandhi, had given up his British citizenship and become a naturalized Indian citizen after independence in 1947. He had returned to Cambridge and studied anthropology. Then, renouncing his missionary calling, Montforce had turned his back on the church, become an anthropologist, and married a tribal girl. Prime Minister Nehru later appointed him "Advisor to the Government of India for Tribal Affairs."

Ro had never personally met Dr. Montforce, but knew of his work among the tribals from having read most of the former missionary's nearly twenty books on the tribes of northeast India. These books had fired Ro's desire to help his tribal people.

The second man who influenced him was Dr. Bob Pierce, an American. Pierce had been with *Youth for Christ* and later started a missionary relief work. Ro went to a "youth night" program of YFC to hear the tall, blond American pour out his heart in sadness over the misery he had just witnessed in Korea.

When the YFC director took up an offering for the suffering people in Korea, Ro gave his last rupees.

Although he did not meet Bob Pierce then, Ro included the American in his prayers regularly as a result of that program. The sincere compassion for suffering people shown by the American deeply affected him.

Ro successfully completed his studies at St. Paul's College in Calcutta and earned an intermediate degree. His government scholarship allowed him to enter the University of Allahabad in the fall of 1952. He clearly remembered how he had walked ninety-six miles through the jungle to begin his education at Churachandpur grammar school. After that, he'd gone to high school in Assam and then attended St. Paul's College. Now, after several delays, he was enrolled at the University of Allahabad in the united province called "Uttarpradesh," some 400 miles southeast of Delhi, in the north central region of the country.

At the university, Ro discovered he could no longer go by the name "Rochunga, son of Chawnga, of the Manipur hills." He decided to adopt the name *Pudaite.* "I am Rochunga of the Leiri clan of the Hmars," Ro said proudly. Then using the name of Pudai, a famous ancestor, he wrote *Pudaite* on his entrance form, meaning "descendant of Pudai."

At the university Ro quickly became active in spreading his faith. One day while he was putting Christian tracts under doors in a dormitory, an Indian student, wearing a turban, slacks, and a sweater, emerged from one of the rooms. He picked up the tract Ro had just slipped under his door.

"Stop, there!" he called, holding up the tract. "Is this your doing?"

"Yes," Ro said, walking back to meet the Indian student. "I am Rochunga Pudaite."

The turbanned student looked at Ro closely. "I am Indian," he said proudly. "Are you Indian?"

Ro nodded. "I am a Hmar tribesman and citizen of India." The student looked intently at Ro's oriental features, so strikingly different from his dark-skinned face.

"I am from the state of Manipur," Ro added. He then pointed to the tract held by the student. "This will tell you how you can have eternal life."

The Indian student's voice dripped hate. "White missionary dung!" he snarled.

Ro took the rebuff with quiet reassurance. "I have never met a missionary. I am a follower of Jesus Christ."

"You lie! All Indian Christians are converts! We got rid of Jesus Christ when we got rid of the British. You think just because you are a jungle boy you can peddle your crap? We will not have it!"

"I am here to study," Ro said quietly. "I cannot afford to be angry with you." But the student had already whirled around and walked to his room. The door slammed to punctuate his feelings for Ro's evangelistic efforts.

Of the 5,000 students at the University of Allahabad, there were only twenty-two Christians. They had formed SMM, Student Missionary Movement, which Ro attended and unsuccessfully tried to make evangelistic.

"You saw how you were treated when you handed out tracts in your dormitory," one of the students reminded him. "It's a lonely enough life here at school without alienating our friends. We insult them by preaching Christianity. They are convinced that it's a 'white man's religion' fostered by the British."

Ro also found he was in a decided minority in the classroom. Hindu and Muslim professors were highly intelligent and offered solid philosophical arguments for their religious beliefs. In fact, Ro knew that they understood their arguments better than he knew the Bible. He went to the library and read widely from the world's great philosophers, such as Descartes, Voltaire, and Spinoza, as well as the Eastern mystics. For him, the result was confusion.

The Hmar student returned to his room and began to study the Bible. It was the Bible that made things clear and logical. As his theological and philosophical doubts disappeared, he grew more and more confident in his faith and understanding. In his second year at the university, he studied debating. Later he volunteered to take part in a debate sponsored by the philosophy department on the topic: "Should religion be introduced in the university?"

Ro entered the debate hall, which was already filled. A fairly large audience faced a small narrow stage, which had chairs for the debaters. Ro took his seat and listened attentively to the other speakers. Finally, it was his turn.

There was polite applause when Ro was introduced. "I want to say, 'Thank you' to the Department of Comparative Religion and to Professor Benerjee for permitting me a part in this debate," he said. "From fellow students tonight, I have learned many beautiful things. . . .

"Of the beautiful philosophy from the Bhagavad Gita . . . of the wise and beautiful sayings of Buddha in Dammapada . . . of the strong and courageous teaching from the Koran. So I want to say, 'Thank you.'

"But I do not feel that my fellow students want to say, 'Thank you' to me for the beautiful teachings of Jesus in the Bible."

There was a murmur from the students, who were mainly Hindus and Muslims. Ro, appearing not to notice, resumed his speaking. Most of the sounds of disapproval faded as he talked.

"My tribe is mostly Christian. Two generations. With *no* help from white missionaries. In former times in my tribe, we cut off the heads of our enemies. Now, we *pray* for our enemies. In former times in our tribe, we made slaves of weaklings. Now we help to make weaklings strong.

"Suicide in former times? In my tribe, many, *many* took their own lives. But now, hardly ever. The changes did not come from white colonialists. The changes did not come from whips and guns, but from a book!"

Ro won the debate. Increasingly, he was aware of the power of the Bible. Without a single white missionary's help beyond the five-day appearance by Watkin Roberts, almost a half-century before, the *majority of the 100,000 Hmars* had converted from spirit worship to the Christian faith. The progressive changes in the jungles and mountains on the part of the Hmars had come entirely from practicing the teachings of Jesus Christ.

However, Ro was once again tempted to abandon his goal and enter business. He received a letter from his old friend, Prasad:

It has been a long time since we were street vendors, Rochunga. It is important that I see you on my next trip to Allahabad.

Prasad specified a restaurant for their meeting. When Prasad and Ro met, they followed an Indian up the ornate steps of an exclusive restaurant in Allahabad. The Indian was much taller than both of them. He wore a red jacket and white turban, the immaculate native costume of a mâitre d' used to being around wealthy people. His practiced eye instantly noted Ro's shabby clothing. The Indian's air of condescension was all but subdued. Prasad's impeccable handtailored Western suit assured the mâitre d' that at least one of the diners "belonged," and could obviously pay well for himself and his poorer friend. Ro felt out of place in the expensive restaurant.

Prasad and Ro were seated at a small round table resplendent with white linen and fine silverware. After the waiter took the order, Prasad launched into his rapid, lilting English. "I was a student once, so I know what it feels like to

Ten-year-old Ro fords a river on his way to begin school at Churachandpur. Scene from the film *Beyond the Next Mountain*

Upper left: Ro as a teenager

Upper right: Ro in 1953 when a student at the University of Allahabad

Bottom: Ro and the beloved "Dr. Bob" (Dr. Bob Pierce), who encouraged and supported Ro and his translation work

Chawnga dedicating a copy of Ro's translation of the Bible into the Hmar language. Scene from the film *Beyond the Next Mountain*

Top: Ro and Mawii on their wedding day, January 1, 1959

Bottom: Ro and Mawii mailing a New Testament soon after Bibles for the World was organized

Top: Chawnga and Daii Pudaite with their children and grand-children in 1979. Photo by John L. Pudaite

Middle: Ro with his parents, Chawnga and Daii, and his older brother, Ramlien, in 1979. Photo by John L. Pudaite

Bottom: Portrait of the Rochunga Pudaite family in 1980: (left to right: Paul, Mawii, Mary, Ro, and John)

Top: Bibles for the World international headquarters, Wheaton, Illinois

Bottom: Ro holding a telephone receiver—symbolic of his vision to reach the entire world for Christ

crave a good meal. Yes, I was a *student*—of accounting. I even got a degree with first-class honors. I became an accountant, but there were no positions for accountants.

"Tonight, my dear Rochunga, my dear, dear friend, you are *my* guest! No more sitting in stalls, those dirty little *tabas*, and all those hawking cries!"

Prasad raised his voice in imitation, calling out in Bengali some of the products he and Ro had once sold. Two of the other diners seated nearby looked up in amusement.

Both Ro and Prasad laughed in recollection. Prasad shook out his napkin and placed it carefully over the fine British woolen suit he wore. Ro watched uncomfortably, then imitated his old friend. He had never been coached on how to behave in such an elegant setting. Ro carefully noted which fork Prasad chose from the glittering array beside his plate.

"Now," Prasad continued, "I just pick up the telephone and call my customers long distance. I've got customers in Karachi, New Delhi, Bombay, and even Tehran. Customers that I've never even seen, Rochunga. Can you imagine?"

Prasad was beside himself with delight. He paused, looking across the table at Ro. "We're still friends, eh, Rochunga?" Prasad asked. Ro nodded and Prasad smiled, taking a mouthful of food.

"We made good money together, eh, Rochunga?" Prasad hesitated a second, then laid down his fork. Leaning across the table, he said intently, "Look, there's a job I can offer you with a house, a car, a percentage of profits." Without waiting for Ro's reaction, he asked, "Well, does that please you?"

Ro's face showed internal struggle. He had left his jungle village many years ago in order to study enough to translate the Bible into Hmar. Now, Prasad was offering the temptation to turn aside again.

When Ro didn't answer immediately, Prasad wiped his fingers on the spotless white cloth napkin and lightly ran his hands over his Western-style pinstriped suit and expensive silk tie. "My business is growing by leaps and bounds,

Rochunga," he stated simply. "Can we be *partners* again?"

Ro quietly replied, "I am offered a scholarship to study. . . ."

Prasad's voice rose angrily. "Study? Do you want to be a student *all* your life?"

"I want to—I want to learn the Greek language, the Hebrew language."

Prasad exploded. "The Greek language! The Hebrew language! You can study in your spare time!"

With difficulty, the Hindu businessman regained control of his emotions. He continued softly, "Rochunga, when I was a little boy, I was told that everything in life was measured and that the world was an illusion. Then when I got my degree with first-class honors, I couldn't get a job for which I was qualified.

"So I took up work as a kitchen boy, you know? I was paid so little that I picked up scraps from the rubbish heap just to stay alive!

"I soon realized that the things of this world are *not* illusion." He paused and looked into the troubled eyes of his young friend. "Together, we could become *rich*, Rochunga."

Prasad's voice had sunk to a whisper, burdened with the weight of his emotions. He looked across the table. For a long while neither man spoke.

"Do I at least tempt you, Rochunga?"

Ro swallowed hard, his thoughts spinning. He loved business. As a small boy in grammar school, he had seen that money was necessary for survival, even for so noble a purpose as becoming educated enough to translate the Bible. His thoughts recalled the years of his milking cows twice daily and of trading in his village. Selling cigarettes in wartime and bartering needles and shirts and malaria pills and razor blades had taught him many lessons. The memories spun through Ro's mind. What Prasad was saying seemed worthwhile, logical.

Ro had repeatedly tried to get out of completing the Bible translation, but his parents had been adamant in their prayers that he continue. Yet, to him, the easiest, most enjoyable thing he could do was sell something, trade something, do anything with a business connection. Was Prasad tempting him?

"Yes," Ro replied slowly, truthfully.

"Well, then, what do you say?"

Ro hesitated. At the start of the conversation, Prasad had offered him a job. Now he was being offered a full partnership and an opportunity to become rich. Years ago, his father had told him that Satan, like the rogue elephant, would tempt him, trying to lure Ro from the objective to which he had committed his life. "How will I know when I am tempted, my father?" Ro had asked. *"You will know, my son,"* his father had said.

Ro now looked across the table at his friend.

"I do not say what Rochunga is to do; *God* says. God says and I obey."

"God? *God?*" Prasad's voice was choked with hissing anger. "Where was God when we were dining on the rubbish heap?" The Indian businessman caught himself and asked softly, "How can anyone know God? I mean, he's so infinite. . . ."

". . . Jesus went hungry like you, Prasad!" Ro interrupted quietly. "God became Jesus so he could become close to you, suffer like you, and understand how you feel."

Ro hesitated, looking earnestly across the table at his friend, then added, "You need a business partner? Take in Jesus as your partner—in your heart."

Prasad was silent.

Ro asked, "Do you have a Bible, Prasad?"

"No."

"I will *send* you a Bible, Prasad, in the English language. I want you to read it."

Prasad gazed across the table at Ro. A Bible wasn't what Prasad wanted. He didn't want to know about so abstract a concept as God, the Infinite, the Unknowing, the Unknowable. Prasad wanted a practical business partner with a keen sense of the commercial, someone who knew the value of buying low and selling high, someone who knew that money spelled *power*.

It was obvious that Ro, although having all the right qualities, was not going to join him. Finally, Prasad sighed deeply and regretfully. Slowly, he nodded in understanding and finished his meal.

EIGHT
MEETINGS OF THE PROVIDENTIAL KIND

Ro was now feeling stronger in his commitment to God's purposes than at any other time in his life. Once the decision had been firmed up in his mind, all of his activities and involvements began falling into place. He no longer felt torn between a business career and his responsibility to his father and his people. Business would simply have to wait.

In his desire to help his people in more material ways, he was also eager to inform the prime minister that the Hmars had been overlooked in the national census. His initial correspondence with Nehru's office had led to his getting a college scholarship, so, Ro reasoned, a personal meeting with the great statesman could also get tangible help for his tribe. But how? New Delhi was 400 miles from Allahabad, and Ro was certain that it would be impossible to see Nehru without an appointment.

Ro learned that Nehru's home, Anandbhavan, was not far from Allahabad. He waited until a working committee of Nehru's All India Congress political party convened at Anandbhavan. Ro decided to try to see Nehru at his home.

Ro borrowed a Western-style suit jacket, put on his best

shirt and tie, and walked up to the prime minister's residence.

"Your pass, please," the sentry snapped.

"I—I am here to see the prime minister," Ro stammered.

"You must have a pass. I am sorry."

"But I *must* see the prime minister. I am a citizen of India; it is my right."

"Only if you have a pass," the guard answered briskly.

Ro had an idea. He waited for the changing of the guard and the posting of a new sentry at the gate. Ducking into some bushes, he began to remove his jacket, tie, and shirt. He took off his pants and shoes. Then, he wrapped his colorful *puon* around his waist and threw a second *puon* over his shoulders.

With renewed confidence Rochunga strode quickly back to the gate of the prime minister's residence. With a voice full of authority, Ro loudly announced, "I have come from the hills of Manipur to see the prime minister!"

"I am sorry, sir, but I cannot admit you without a pass," the sentry replied.

Ro felt frustrated and helpless. But at that moment, a cabinet minister, Lal Bahadur Shastri, came by and noticed him in tribal dress. "Mr. Nehru is taking a short rest just now," he explained. "But perhaps you would like to see his daughter, Indira Gandhi?"

Ro was led to an outside veranda of the huge residence where he met Mrs. Gandhi, who asked him to sit and talk. Mrs. Gandhi listened intently for nearly an hour as Ro told her about the Hmar tribe and the other tribal people in the hills that had neither government schools nor post offices.

"Do you have this information in writing?" she asked.

Thoroughly prepared for this meeting, Ro assured her that he did. He took out the typewritten report and handed it to her.

"You must give this to my father," she said and led him inside the mansion.

To Ro, a former jungle boy reared in a bamboo hut, the

prime minister's receiving room seemed awe-inspiring. Ro stood barefooted on the white marble floor. Two immense white couches dominated the room. An overhead fan circulated the humid air in the large room while Prime Minister Jawaharlal Nehru, wearing his famous white cap, reclined on one of the spotless couches.

Nehru's daughter introduced Ro and briefly explained the purpose of his visit. She gave her father Ro's typewritten report, which he scanned. As he read, Ro shuffled uncomfortably. His eyes roamed the room, glancing at the immense library in the next room and the tasteful decor and artifacts displayed on polished antique wood furniture.

When the prime minister finally looked up, he smiled and spoke, his words rising and falling in the rapid manner of Indians speaking English. "Not included in the national census?"

"No, sir," Ro replied, adding, "and there are many Hmar villages, sir."

"How many of you are there? Oh, but then, how would you know when you've not been counted?" the prime minister said, answering his own question.

"Pardon, sir. The Hmar tribe and neighboring tribes inhabit a territory of 4,000 square miles. A *4,000* square-mile territory with no government school. Four-thousand miles with no post office! My father must walk on foot eighty miles—a journey of three or four days—just to receive my letter."

"Oh, dear! Look here. Do me a favor? Leave all this information before you go. May I keep this report? I promise you I shall study it."

"Yes. Thank you, sir." Ro bowed politely, then turned to leave, but the prime minister's voice caught him and brought him back.

"Ah, say! Look here! You're a bright chap. We need to educate bright young men like you. We need them for government posts in tribal areas. I want you to leave me your name and address. There's always a place in government service for young men with your abilities and compassion for the people."

Ro retained an air of dignity until he got outside. When he reached the vast lawns, however, he began running and then jumped in a joyous tribal dance of delight.

Perhaps God is arranging things in my life so that I can enter politics or government service upon completion of the translation, he thought. Ro toyed with the idea. He remembered the first time he'd seen the provincial governor. Ro had been in Churachandpur elementary school when all the beautiful government tents had been pitched in the village. The great pomp and ceremony had thoroughly impressed Ro as a boy.

Since then, he'd often thought how much good *he* could do for his people if he were in politics. That was the ultimate place of influence; people in politics had the power to *do* things. There were also fame and glory, along with other wonderful benefits—houses, cars, and travel. None of that was available in the simple, plain Hmar villages.

Now, with his first exposure to the government, a tribal boy had met with India's top chief executive. *Yes,* Ro thought, *I am certain now that after the translation is complete, I will become a politician, perhaps even a governor!*

Ro made the long trip home to tell his parents. His father and mother rejoiced most that Ro was solidly committed to his original goal.

"You are on God's path, my son," Daii said to Rochunga. "I am happy."

"Yes, mother. At last I have peace in my soul for this matter also. I am praying that God will open for me a door to the West to study overseas. I must study Hebrew and Greek in order to translate the Bible."

"Your father and I will pray also," she replied. "And Rochunga," she added with a twinkle in her eye, "we will pray that God gives you a wife."

While in the village, Ro had been somewhat aware of how many of the young men his age were already married and rearing families. He had not thought much about it until his mother's comment. "But surely, mother, I am far too busy, and my life is too complicated to take a wife just now," he told her.

"When you are on God's path, he will lead," was all she said.

Later, during the school vacation, Ro taught a class in English for young people of the tribe. Only the most dedicated ones took part, for the class met at six in the morning. I was one of those attending.

Ro's eyes roamed across the students, then stopped when they came to me. I was several years younger than he. I was wrapped in a red and black *puon* against the early morning chill. Ro could not take his eyes off me.

She is almost five feet tall, slender, and perfectly proportioned. Her flowing black hair accents her dark eyes and light brown skin so beautifully, Ro thought. He knew instinctively that many young Hmar men would soon be sending their representatives to call on my father or older brothers.

In the Hmar custom, the visitor would bring a pot of tea, a short-handled hoe, and other gifts. The whole village would then know that a suitor was beginning negotiations to arrange a marriage. The entire village would also know the outcome by what the representative had in his hands when he returned from the girl's bamboo hut.

If he carried away every item with which he had entered, that meant that the father had vetoed even a meeting between his daughter and the suitor. If the representative left without the pot of tea and hoe, then the father had allowed the tea to be boiled and drunk. In the old days, before many Hmars had become Christians, there had been rice beer, but believers had switched to tea. If the hoe were left, then the father was considering the marriage proposal. Keeping the short-handled hoe was an invitation to return and continue the negotiations.

Yes, it will not be long, Ro thought, still looking at me, *before suitors send their representatives to her father to discuss marriage.*

Ro's eyes caught mine. It was not proper for a Hmar girl to flirt or even to let a Hmar boy know her feelings, but for just a fraction of a second, I had let the ghost of a smile touch my lips as I returned his gaze.

Rochunga had no time to dwell on thoughts of romance, however. Soon he would have to go back to the university for his final year of study in India and pray that God would permit him to study abroad.

Back at the university, everything was going well for Ro. Then one morning, he awoke with severe stomach cramps. A doctor diagnosed the problem as acute appendicitis. "There is no time to waste, young man. You must have surgery at once!"

"But—but I have no money for the hospital or an operation," Ro stammered.

The doctor shook his head gravely. "You *must* find 150 rupees somewhere before your appendix ruptures. It will kill you!"

Ro got dressed and thanked the doctor, then walked slowly outside, feeling more depressed and frightened than he ever had before. He had already used his father's last rupees for school. His own funds were gone and his part-time employment paid only enough for school incidentals. There was no time to find other work and earn enough for the operation and hospital expenses. Also he could think of no one from whom he could borrow the money. It seemed like a hopeless situation. What could he do?

In desperation, Ro prayed, "Lord, I know of no way to get 150 rupees. It is an impossible amount of money. But I will trust you. If it is necessary for me to have this operation, my life is in your hands. *You* will have to supply the money!"

Rochunga had been helping with the publicity for an upcoming YFC rally organized by area director Cyril Thompson. Ro planned to tell him he could no longer help promote the rally featuring Bob Pierce. He would not be able to pedal his bicycle, let alone hang posters all over town as originally planned.

Ro was surprised to meet Bob Pierce at the Thompsons when he went to break the news. "I was most impressed with your message in Calcutta," Ro told the tall American.

"Well, thank you, brother," Pierce grinned. "It's good to meet you. Tell me about yourself."

Ro forgot about his stomach pain as he told the story of his tribe and explained that almost all of his people were now Christians. Pierce was visibly moved by the account.

"What are you doing now?" he asked Ro.

"I am preparing to study so that I can translate the Bible into the language of the Hmar people."

"That's wonderful," the American missionary leader replied. "Well, let me pray for you before I go."

Bob Pierce towered nearly a foot above Ro; his deep voice seemed to fill the house. He prayed long and earnestly for his new friend Ro. Then he put his arms around him in a bear hug and walked to the door.

"I've got to leave now," he said. "God bless you, brother," he told Ro. The young man felt him slip something into his shirt pocket.

When he was alone later, Ro looked into his pocket. There were *150 rupees,* enough for his operation! But how could the American have known? Ro had said nothing about his appendicitis to the missionary. *God knew,* Ro reminded himself.

The next morning Ro went to the hospital and was operated on. When the effects of the anesthesia wore off, the doctor told him, "Young man, it's a good thing you came when you did. The operation was successful, but you'd have never lasted the week!"

Later, after recovering from the surgery, Ro heard that Bob Pierce was in India to make a film. He decided to thank Pierce personally for saving his life.

When the two later met, the American dismissed his role.

"I only follow God's leading, buddy. Praise the Lord, not me."

Pierce invited Ro to go with him for a weekend rally in Calcutta. The delightful chance to visit the city where he had studied and to spend time getting to know Bob Pierce was too much to refuse.

As they talked, Bob Pierce sensed the need to encourage Ro in his sincere purpose. "How would you like to go abroad for further study? I think it would help your translation work if you could study in Britain or the United States," Pierce suggested.

"I can think of nothing better than this," Ro admitted and told Pierce of his own prayers toward that end.

"Well, it might take a long time for you to get a passport. You ought to apply now. I'll see if World Vision will sponsor your studies overseas."

While Ro prayed about the unique opportunity God was giving him, God was also working within my own life in the hills of Manipur. My parents had named me Lalrimawi, meaning "the name of the Lord is a beautiful sound." Most people called me "Mawii" for short. I was the youngest of eight children growing up in a godly tribal home. Both my parents were deeply committed Christians, who sought God's best for me and my siblings. They had sent me to a nearby village elementary school, a half-day's walk from our village.

The nearest advanced [high] school was a three-day journey through the jungle. Few teenaged girls went to advanced school. Most remained in the village to prepare for marriage.

I, however, had not been interested in marriage, praying for an education with which to serve God. I was grateful that my father understood my motivation and never seriously entertained the suitors who sent him tea and hoes.

Even as a young girl I had considered the marriage customs less than satisfactory. A girl had little to say. The parents arranged the marriage, and it didn't matter much if the girl did not like the suitor. I remember hoping that my father would let me marry not only someone I truly loved, but also someone with a similar desire to serve God. Both of my parents were sensitive to my desire to serve God and follow his will.

My older sister, Rikhum, was the wife of a teacher-evangelist. Some years earlier, Ro had visited her husband's school. Rikhum came home to tell me about Ro's visit.

"He is very bright and handsome," she said. "And he loves God. I thought when I met him, *Oh, if someday Mawii might meet him.*"

"But, U Rikhum," I had giggled, "he is *old.* He is probably more than twenty!"

"That is not so old. Wait a few years and you will see."

Rikhum and I were very close. I was thankful for her leading me to Christ just two years before. Rikhum was delighted to see me hungering for spiritual things. "Your prayers and devotional times are more mature than those of many adult believers, Mawii," she said to me.

When I was about fourteen, I had met Rochunga for the first time. On his vacation from school, he had come to teach English at the village school I was attending. The teenagers called him "U Rochunga," a term of respect like "older brother." U Rochunga also preached on Saturday night in services of the tribal church. It was at church that I was smitten with him.

I was impressed, as had been Rikhum, with Ro's ability and personality. But it was his preaching that genuinely moved me. Months later I could still remember what he had said—practically word for word.

That night I knelt beside my bed and prayed for a long time, thinking about the pressures I was facing from friends and neighbors to entertain suitors. I wrinkled up my nose at the thought. "Boys are such a nuisance," I confided to God. "Lord, if you ever want me to get married in days to come when I am older, I pray you will give me a young man like U Rochunga, who loves you, Lord." Then I added a postscript: "Meanwhile, Lord, please keep those boys away from our house so I can study."

Before Ro went back to Allahabad, he encouraged the students to finish their secondary schooling and go on to college. "The Lord needs trained Christian leaders," Ro had told me and the other teenaged students. At that time there were few good schools and colleges in northeast India, so Ro had recommended a specific school for me. "St. Mary's is a school in Shillong, accepting only female students," he said. "You should attend and get a college degree."

I later enrolled at St. Mary's. Ro was right about the school. My older brother, Khuma, was studying in the same city. The teachers—nuns from Canada, Australia, and England—taught English very well.

When Ro got word that I was the first girl of our Hmar tribe to graduate from high school and enter college, he wrote to me at St. Mary's. I felt quite lonely at college. When Ro's first letter came, I didn't tell any of my classmates. Instead, I quickly went to a room for privacy and read it before the Lord.

I was very far from my home, and while the students with whom I lived were nice, I didn't feel free to share some things with them. So I went to the Lord with my personal joys and thoughts. The Lord and I had a very close relationship.

I began to pray, "Lord, how shall I answer? Please help me write the letter." I knew that I had to be discreet— as was expected of a Hmar girl—and not let him detect any fondness or attraction, but I also wanted to correspond with him!

Finally I began to write, addressing him as "Dear U Rochunga," the proper form of address for a teacher by a student. I closed the letter as I had begun—discreetly. I signed it with my full name, "Lalrimawi."

Some weeks later, at St. Mary's, I approached the large iron grill gate as the Indian mailman handed letters through the iron bars to the girls under the watchful eye of the supervising nun. I tried to control my excitement.

"Hlawngwi," the mailman called, handing a letter through the bars to a teenaged girl, who eagerly took it. The mailman handed the same girl a second letter and then gave one to the nun. The letters kept coming. Then the mailman turned and started to walk away.

Disappointment covered my face.

The postman turned back to the iron gate. "Oh, Sister! Here is one more." He extended another letter through the bars. The nun accepted it, glanced at the name, and then smilingly handed it over to me.

I waited to read it in an empty classroom, hearing Ro's voice through the written words:

Dear Mawii,
Thank you for answering my letter so warmly. I am very pleased that you are seeking a higher education, as I am. Here I am working hard to complete my education. I am very thankful to God for this opportunity. . . .

The letter had a few items of tribal news and some remarks about his work. It closed with affection and prayers for my studies at St. Mary's.

When Ro read my next letter, he told me, he could clearly hear my voice in every line:

Dear U Rochunga,
Please do not think my letters are only a schoolgirl's way to practice writing English. There is one person I write to and pray for always, and it is Rochunga.

If it pleases you, continue to write English letters to me, as you have, and it will please me to continue to answer.

I feel privileged to be the first Hmar girl ever to leave

the jungles to seek an education in the outside world. It is because of God's direct leading and your fine example, U Rochunga.

Ro was pleased, of course. He thought, *I met Mawii in the village when she was only fourteen or fifteen. I knew suitors would soon be coming around. She has defied one tradition already by going off to school. Perhaps she can hold out against the marriage suitors as well.* I did, in fact, manage to put off the marriage suitors!

Ro and I began corresponding more and more frequently, although neither of us allowed the "pleasant distraction" to interfere with the principal goal of completing our education.

NINE
"GLASGOW!
GLASGOW! GLASGOW!"

Just as Ro was completing his last year of studies at the
university, he received a letter from the secretary to Prime
Minister Nehru:

*The prime minister will be pleased to grant you an
appointment on Tuesday next, at 3:00 P.M. to discuss
your qualifications for a government post to the tribal
areas.*

Ro was proud and delighted. He still had heard nothing
about his passport application and wondered if getting one
was even possible. So, as a backup plan, Ro considered the
prospect of government work with its opportunities for
quick advancement by a "sharp young man." He had written for the appointment with Nehru, not really expecting an
answer. But now that the reply had come, was it not God's
way of telling him to enter government service? It had been
a "fleece" of sorts. He had prayed that the door to government service not even open—if that were God's will.

But what now? The door was not only opening, but also
swinging wide for him to pass through!

The prime minister spoke earnestly to Ro when he arrived

in New Delhi on Tuesday. "We have to be careful about appointing officers anywhere, but even more so in the tribal areas."

Ro remained silent as Nehru paused, then resumed his conversation.

"Now you, as a tribal person, should eminently qualify. I will personally recommend you and forward your application to the man in charge of tribal affairs. He will then grant you an interview." Ro knew the man would be Dr. Alan Montforce, the naturalized Indian and former Anglican missionary.

Nehru continued, "You realize, of course, that the final decision will lie with Dr. Montforce."

Prime Minister Nehru personally introduced Ro to Dr. Montforce, who happened to be visiting in New Delhi. Ro noted that the director of tribal affairs was tall, nice-looking, amiable, and quite Western in appearance, despite his Indian dress. After a pleasant chat, Dr. Montforce requested that Ro come to his office in Shillong for an official interview the following Saturday.

After his regular Saturday afternoon Bible study with some tribal students, Ro went straight to Montforce's for the interview. It was already dark by the time Ro alighted from the black limousine which had been provided for him. He was neatly dressed in a dark Western suit with starched white shirt and subdued tie. He knew he would be dealing with a former British official and wanted to make the right impression.

"Welcome!" Montforce said cheerfully. "Welcome indeed, Mr. Pu-die-tay," he said, pronouncing the name slowly. "I do hope I'm pronouncing that correctly."

Ro nodded, still standing. "Yes. Yes, sir."

"It's not a family name, I understand. It really means 'descendant of Pudai.'"

"That is correct, sir."

"Well, it makes a perfectly splendid surname. Do sit down,

please. Would you care for a drink? Some fruit juice? Whiskey?"

"Fruit juice, please." Ro sat down on a dark sofa, feeling nervous.

Montforce continued talking to his tribal guest while he poured himself a jigger of whiskey from a small bar against the wall. "Yes, a little chilly in the evenings this time of year, isn't it?"

Ro nodded. Montforce raised his glass, sipped, and then got down to business. "Well, Mr. Pudaite, you come to me very highly recommended. The prime minister himself tells me good things about you. You know, that pleases me as well, because we need qualified political officers in our tribal areas. And your being a tribal yourself, well, that's a huge advantage. Yes, the responsibilities are numerous, but there are a number of rewards, as well."

An attractive tribal woman reappeared with a large glass of fruit juice. "Pardon me, Alan," she said, "I thought I'd bring this in myself."

"Oh, thank you, darling. Mr. Pudaite, this is my wife." The two exchanged greetings.

She said, "The fruit juice is yours, I'm sure, Mr. Pudaite."

"Thank you." Ro had stood for the introductions. He took the glass and remained standing as Mrs. Montforce turned to her husband.

"Alan, I hope I'm not interrupting?"

"No, of course not. Sit down." He raised his glass to Ro. "Well, good health. Oh, and please, have a seat, Mr. Pudaite."

Ro raised his glass in imitation of his host and sipped his drink, then sat on the edge of the sofa.

"I was just about to mention to Mr. Pudaite the profits of the position we're discussing. Now," he said, turning to Ro, "besides a more-than-adequate salary, you'll have an allowance for a bungalow, servants, even a car!"

Ro set his glass down on the coffeetable and grinned broadly. "That pleases me very much! Such generous rewards for serving tribal people!"

Mrs. Montforce chuckled softly.

Dr. Montforce's obvious pleasure at Ro's qualifications made his enthusiasm grow as he looked at Ro again. He studied the file in front of him.

"I see that you've studied in Calcutta and Allahabad. Now that is remarkable for a tribal, isn't it, dear?" he commented to his wife.

Ro said quietly, "Prayers of my parents were answered."

Looking up, Montforce noticed for the first time the large black Bible on Ro's lap. There was an instant, but subtle, reaction in Montforce's face. He studied Ro silently for a moment, then asked, "Uh, did you study anthropology, by any chance? That's my field."

Ro answered, "No, sir. Philosophy . . . religion. It was not always easy. Only a few Christians at the university, but God was good."

Mrs. Montforce saw a twitch in her husband's face and knew it was time to change the subject. "Would you like more fruit juice, Mr. Pudaite?"

"No, thank you," Ro answered. Now he was aware of the tension which had suddenly replaced the warm atmosphere, but he was unaware of its cause.

Ro continued his explanation, "I study the Bible much. It helped me with the English language. Someday it is my prayer to translate the Bible into the Hmar language."

The pleased and proud announcement had an exactly opposite effect on the host. He finished his whiskey and held out the glass to his wife. "Darling, would you please?" She rose quickly, took the glass, and moved silently toward the bar.

Montforce's voice was distinctly cool as he asked, "You wish to translate the Bible for your people?"

"Yes, but I will have to study sources in the Hebrew and Greek languages."

"Quite an undertaking, I'm sure." Montforce took the refilled glass from his wife and sipped it slowly. Then with some resignation he continued, "Well, Mr. Pudaite. I should should have suspected from the way you came dressed, but it seems—it seems that in my enthusiasm to enlist qualified personnel, I am guilty of overlooking certain things about you, Mr. Pudaite." Montforce quickly looked at his wife and then disapprovingly at Ro before adding softly, "I am most certainly. We can't have you carrying your Bible to the tribes in the northeast India frontier area!" He stood up.

He took a few slow steps, his heels echoing on the hardwood floor. "It comes as a great disappointment to me to discover that you are a *mission native.*" His voice had the same tone of scorn and disapproval Ro had heard when distributing tracts at the university. He had not expected it here from a former missionary.

Montforce raised his voice. "Some ignorant, ill-informed, short-sighted white missionaries have ruined you!"

Ro protested, "Sir, to the Hmar tribe *ever*, came only *one* white missionary!"

"All right, *one!* Well, *he*'s turned you out looking like something out of Bond Street or Saville Row!"

Ro stood abruptly. "Dr. Montforce!" He paused, calming his own voice in the ways he had been taught in addressing an elder. "Sir, missionary Roberts came to our hills *before I was born!* He lived with our tribe like a brother."

"I don't believe that!"

"He was preparing himself to translate the Bible into the Hmar language, but the British Raj drove him out!"

"Yes, certainly! Guns and Gospels! The British took this land with guns and Gospels! Happily, at least the guns have been withdrawn!"

Mrs. Montforce interrupted her husband. "Alan, may I remind you that there's freedom of religion in this country?"

Her husband replied, "That is not the issue."

She persisted, "If Mr. Pudaite is qualified. . . ."

". . . Ruth!" He interrupted her with restrained firmness. "Alan, if he is qualified. . . ."

"Excuse me, Dr. Montforce. If I cannot carry my Bible

with me, I will not accept this appointment," Ro said.

Montforce looked surprised and annoyed by Ro's bold statement. "As—as you wish," he stammered.

Ro quietly left the house and went back to the waiting car. His face reflected the pain of the unjust event which had dashed his hopes of serving his people in a government post. Tears slowly welled in his eyes, then slid down his cheeks. Ro buried his face in his hands. Sobs shook his body as the car sped to his hotel in Shillong.

For Ro, it was one of the darkest moments he was ever to experience.

Ro returned to his native Manipur. Instead of going home, he went to Imphal City for a few days. Even though he now held degrees from St. Paul's College and Allahabad University, the honors could not quite overshadow the bitter disappointment of his encounter with Montforce. Only time would ease his grief.

While in Imphal he wrote to his parents, asking them to pray for God's direction: "I do not know what God wants me to do. Please pray that I will not miss his best."

At his hotel in Imphal, Ro sat chatting with two friends from his tribe when a uniformed government messenger arrived. All eyes watched as the messenger walked over to Ro's table.

"Are you Rochunga Pudaite?" he asked.

"Yes. How may I help you?"

The man handed Ro a document with an official seal from the prime minister. Ro opened it and read it, wondering what he had done to warrant a summons.

The document requested his help in selecting both the locations of four post offices in the Hmar area, and the names of four people to serve as postmasters. Ro felt deeply gratified by the unexpected honor the government had just given him. He was pleased to play a small part in opening up his area to the outside world via the postal system.

Ro studied the map of the Manipur state. Then he picked the locations and wrote the names of four people he thought would make good postmasters.

By the time Ro got back to his village, the news of his meeting with the prime minister and the subsequent honor bestowed on him had already preceded him. Ro was greeted as a celebrity of sorts.

Chawnga and Daii welcomed their son, but were also proud of him for another reason. He had completed the studies necessary for the task they had prayed for him to accomplish. He was now closer than ever to the goal of translating God's Word into Hmar.

Ro's fame quickly spread across the Manipur hills. One day he was met by a delegation of people trying to organize a political party among the Hmars. "We have no hospitals, no roads, and no schools of our own," one of the men reminded Ro. "You have met the prime minister. You have won post offices for us. You can help us get other things, too."

At first Ro politely refused, but the organizers were adamant. The group stayed two days to pressure Ro into helping. He finally agreed to serve as organizing chairman of the new party.

"It is yet another way we can help our people," Ro told his father.

"Yes, someone can perhaps do this thing, but it is not your path," Chawnga reminded him. "God has higher plans for you than just as a political leader. The people want you now, but they have short memories. Your fame will not last. They will praise you today, but tomorrow they will curse you. You go to the convention and organize," Chawnga said. "I will go to the mountain and pray for you."

In July, some 200 delegates from the various clans traveled to the village of Parbung. When the organizing business was completed, the group still had to elect a leader. Ro was elected unanimously. Thunderous applause followed, and no other nominees were presented. "Come, now," a delegate told Ro after announcing the news, "come and give us your acceptance speech."

"My—my speech must wait," Ro said quickly. "Please. I will write out something and address the assembly tomorrow night."

Ro spent the entire day rehearsing his thoughts for an acceptance speech. As the time drew near for his address, a runner brought Ro some mail. There were three important letters.

The first was a letter from Indira Gandhi, congratulating him on his plans to help his people. The second letter, also congratulatory, was from the governor of Assam. A third letter, from the University of Allahabad, brought the news he had expected—he had successfully passed his examinations, and his degree certificate would be sent.

There was another piece of mail, actually a cable message, which had been sent to a tribal preacher in another village eighty miles away. The man quickly forwarded it to Ro. The message was from Toronto, Canada, and read:

INFORM ROCHUNGA PUDAITE MY FRIENDS AND I WILL
PAY FOR INTENSIVE BIBLE TRAINING IN GLASGOW OR
LONDON STOP CABLE DECISION

The cable was signed *Watkin R. Roberts*. Ro was stunned. *I did not know that Mr. Young Man even knew I existed*, he thought. He was in a great dilemma. Which way should he go? Should he remain in India and lead this newly formed political party or should he accept Roberts' invitation? At the political convention, he read the letters of congratulations aloud, but said nothing of the cable. The delegates were puzzled, however, when Ro asked to postpone his acceptance speech yet another day.

"We will do as you wish," one of the delegates said. "We are your followers. You will lead the Hmars to national recognition and bring us the benefits of progress. You will be our great and famous leader, Rochunga!"

That night Ro could not sleep. He rose while it was still dark and walked in the moonlight. The night was quite still. Only the crickets and tree frogs stirred. He strolled outside the village, crossed a *jhum*, and finding a small deserted hut nearby, went inside to pray.

For over an hour, Ro prayed: "Lord, I truly want to do your will. I put aside what I wanted when business opportunities were presented to me. Then, I thought I should go into a government service post, but my plans were crushed when Dr. Montforce closed that door. Now, my people cry out for a leader to help them. I believe you have given me gifts—knowledge, wisdom, ambition, ideas—with which to help my people. It all seemed so clear to me yesterday. But now I have the cable from Mr. Young Man. Tell me what to do, Lord. If I turn my back on my people now, the new political party may die, and our people will lose hope and confidence in the new systems of our country. Still, if I remain here, I may never finish the translation work."

Ro put all his passion into his prayer: "Lord, *please*, tell me what to do! I am willing to follow you down either path you choose for me."

He waited quietly, hearing only the night noises. Then, it was as if the crickets and frogs were singing in unison, "*Glasgow, Glasgow, Glasgow!*" Was he imagining it, or was God speaking directly? "Shall I go to Scotland, Lord?"

Yes! The word filled his heart.

Immediately an overwhelming sense of peace swept over his being. There was absolutely no doubt about it. The passport would come, and he would go to Scotland to study.

It was not easy to share his decision with the other delegates. They had prepared the honorary *puondum* (tribal cloth) and the ornate headdress, which had been given in the past to the great Hmar chiefs. As the long feathers of *vakul* (king bird) were placed on his head, Ro prayed for the right words to say.

He explained how the cable had come and how he had

prayed and was convinced God wanted him to study abroad instead of being their leader. It was not easy to change their minds. Reluctantly, however, the delegates released Ro and elected another Hmar, Lungawi, a college student who spoke English.

It was still all an amazing coincidence to Ro. *What prompted the cable from Watkin Roberts?* he wondered. He knew that only God could have so orchestrated the events of his life. With renewed faith he decided to apply for his passport to go to Scotland.

TEN
MR. YOUNG MAN, I PRESUME?

The prized passport and visa came almost immediately after Ro had made plans to attend Glasgow Bible Training Institute in Scotland.

It was something of an occasion. Only a few Hmars had ever traveled outside the country—generally as soldiers in the Indian army. None had ever gone as civilians. Ro looked at the small passport and fingered its pages lovingly. "Truly, this is a miracle," he told Pastor Walter Cortlett of the William Carey Baptist Church in Calcutta.

"That's why I wanted to see you before you left for the British Isles," Reverend Cortlett said to Ro. "Our people want to send you off with a great *bon voyage* party and commission you as our Indian missionary to the West!" Ro took the commission seriously.

When Ro finally boarded a KLM flight to London, he was too excited to sleep on the plane and read from his leather-bound Bible most of the time. After landing at Heathrow Airport in London, Ro then traveled by train to Scotland, watching a strange countryside unfold as the train sped over the rails northward. He was impressed by the fields and farms and by the industrial cities with their factories and hundreds of workers.

Glasgow was an old city, with soot-blackened stone buildings and many automobiles. Ro soon learned he had to be as wary of speeding cars as he had been of tigers in the jungle. Both could do deadly harm if they came upon him.

The school was fairly small, with only about 100 students—young Christians eager for Bible training. At first Ro had a difficult time remembering their names. "Here are all white faces," he wrote home, "and at first I cannot tell one from another."

Principal McBeth at the Bible Training Institute took a keen interest in Ro. "Mr. Pudaite," he said in his Scottish brogue, "you have made significant progress in your studies in India. You are ahead of most of the students here. I'm afraid the classes may not be difficult enough for you. But I have an idea. How would it be if I arranged for you to study Greek and Hebrew at Glasgow University?"

Ro grinned widely. "It is as if you could read my thoughts," he told the principal.

The months went by quickly, and Ro found himself experiencing his first really cold winter. He was unable to afford an overcoat, so the cold rains and icy winds from the North Atlantic made him especially homesick for the lush, green valleys and hills of Manipur.

One day was really remarkable, however. Ro awakened to see the entire outdoors transformed. A clean white blanket had covered everything during the night. In the morning light everything glistened. Ro had never seen such a sight.

"Oh, that's just snow, a bit early this year," he was told casually. Ro excitedly ran out into the yard to touch, hold, and run in it. He threw it into the air and knocked it from the evergreen branches. Naively he took a bucketful into the house to save it, only to watch it melt.

By spring, Ro had begun to get invitations to speak at Scottish churches and evangelistic rallies. Often an honorarium of ten shillings (about $1.35) was given, but that usually went for bus fare, lunch, and other expenses related to the speaking engagement. However, the experiences did give

Ro a chance to practice English, as well as develop his preaching style on others. On other occasions, Ro would go witnessing on the street with other students from the Bible institute.

"I am amazed to find so many who need our Savior," he wrote to his father. "There are drunkards, prostitutes, thieves, and beggars, just as in Calcutta. I am shocked. I was expecting it to be more like heaven here in a country from which so many missionaries have come."

That year, the American evangelist Billy Graham was in Scotland to hold a crusade. Ro adjusted his study load and speaking engagements to do advance work for the Glasgow Crusade. As he had done in Calcutta and Allahabad for Bob Pierce and Youth for Christ meetings, Ro distributed handbills, put up posters, and helped publicize the meetings.

One day, while eating in the dining hall of the Bible institute, he received an unexpected call from one of Billy Graham's aides. "Dr. Graham has heard of you and your efforts and would like to meet you. Can you come to his hotel?" he asked Ro.

"I will be there in five minutes!" Ro announced excitedly and replaced the receiver. He had been too hasty in saying that he would be at the hotel so soon—it was at least two miles away, and he had no transportation. He ran outside and looked in vain for a bus or taxi. Then, without hesitating, he began running in the direction of the hotel. Totally out of breath, he knocked at Graham's hotel door less than fifteen minutes later.

Ro was somewhat awestruck by the American evangelist. He recalled having had the same sense of wonder and shyness when he had first met India's Prime Minister Nehru some years earlier. Billy Graham's casual manner and down-to-earth humility, however, soon eased any sense of awe or intimidation Ro had experienced. The interest Graham showed in the tribal native was friendly and sincere—as genuine as if the conversation had been with a prince or prime minister. Ro felt warmth and brotherly affection pouring out to him during their brief visit.

As they concluded their meeting, Graham asked Ro, "By the way, where are you studying?"

"At the Bible Training Institute," Ro replied.

"Do you plan to stay?"

"No," Ro replied simply. "I have learned what I can there. It is time to move on. I have received an offer of a full scholarship to Oxford University in England."

Dr. Graham asked, "Why don't you come to America?"

Ro could only blink in surprise.

The evangelist added, "I'll make all the necessary arrangements if you want to come to Wheaton College in America to study for your translation work."

Still surprised, Ro could only say, "I will pray about it. Thank you so much for your kindness."

Ro was immediately moved to accept. Bob Pierce, founder of World Vision International, had already offered to sponsor Ro if he wanted to come to America to study. Ro consulted Bob Pierce, who promptly replied:

I do remember that when you were in India I offered you a scholarship to come to America. My offer is still good. I would like you to let Billy Graham arrange your entrance and admission to Wheaton College, and World Vision will take care of the finances. I will have my office send you the money for transportation to America.

Ro received a check for $153 for passage across the Atlantic. It was the figure Ro had given Bob Pierce and Billy Graham for the cost of the cheapest berth on the ocean liner. Unfortunately, the economy fare was also the choice of other students and tourists during the summer. When Ro went to the steamship travel office, he was told that no such accommodations would be available in the foreseeable future.

"Please," Ro told the clerk, "put me on your waiting list, and call me when you have a cancellation."

That was in June. *Surely something will open during the next few weeks so I can travel across the ocean in time to register for classes in September,* Ro thought.

While he waited, Ro began to work on the translation of the Bible into the Hmar language. After many years of preparation, the actual beginning of the task was almost anticlimactic. He started the work quietly, setting aside several hours a day as a regular schedule for the task. He set himself a goal of at least one chapter a day. The translation was made from Greek and Hebrew into English, then from English into Hmar. Next Ro carefully wrote each word out in longhand in a notebook. He worked carefully and revised continuously until he felt the words were right. The translation work continued at a rapid pace since school had ended and Ro was waiting for space on the ocean liner.

By mid-August no boat cancellations had come through. Ro began asking himself, *Did I make the right decision?* He almost regretted having turned down the Oxford scholarship.

On the last Friday of August, Ro became anxious. *I will set aside the entire day to pray about this dilemma,* he determined. Late that afternoon, John Moore, superintendent of the Gospel Tent Hall, knocked on his door. Ro had often participated in the gospel services.

The Gospel Tent Hall Rally, started by evangelist D. L. Moody before the turn of the century, had continued as an evangelistic outreach to the city of Glasgow. Each Saturday evening 3,000 to 4,000 people attended the rally, taking part in the singing and preaching.

"Ro," John Moore said, "I need a favor."

"What is it?" Ro responded.

"The speaker we had scheduled for tomorrow night has suddenly canceled. Would you be kind enough to be my speaker?"

Though flattered by the request, Ro said, "No, John, I cannot. You know my English is not good enough to preach to so many. I cannot do it."

Six-foot-three-inch John Moore—composer of the well-known song, "Burdens are lifted at Calvary. Jesus is very near"—bent down to Ro's eye level. "Take it this way, Ro," he grinned. "You have no reputation to destroy. If you do well, it'll be a great beginning for you. If you don't, who's going to remember?"

"All right," Ro smiled, "I will do it, but you must pray for me."

Ro was nervous the following evening as he looked over the crowd of several thousand. Still somewhat nervous, he began to preach, silently calling upon God to help him. The Holy Spirit responded by giving Ro great ability and effectiveness.

When Ro extended an invitation, fifty-seven persons walked forward to receive Jesus Christ as Savior.

After the meeting, the hall emptied, and Ro returned to the platform to retrieve his notes and Bible. He was unaware that the microphone was still on, and so his remarks carried throughout the hall.

John Moore said to him, "Ro, did I hear you're going to America?"

"Yes," he replied.

"When? How soon do you leave?"

"I—I do not know."

"What do you mean? You're going to America, but you don't know when? I don't understand," Moore said.

"Well, John," Ro explained. "I want to go now. I need to be there soon to enroll in school. But I cannot get a berth on the ship."

In a moment a man walked down the aisle of the huge hall. He came to the front by the platform.

"Excuse me," he said to Ro, "but the public address system picked up what you were saying. I heard you say you couldn't get a berth on the ship crossing the Atlantic. Is that right?"

"Yes," replied Ro glumly.

"Well, can I do anything for you?"

"No," Ro shook his head. "I do not think so. I put my

name on the waiting list, and it has been nearly three months. . . ."

". . . Maybe I can help," the man interrupted.

"You can pray with me," Ro said.

"I think I can do more than pray," the man said. "I'm Alexander Stuart of the Donaldson Line, the largest ship line between Scotland and the New World. In each of our ships, we reserve rooms for last-minute VIP travelers. I'll see that you have a room. . . ."

". . . But, sir," Ro interrupted, "I have only $153 for my ticket."

"It doesn't matter. Leave it to me," Mr Stuart said, scribbling something on the back of one of his business cards. "Give this to the receptionist at the address here, and she'll take care of it."

Ro was delightfully surprised and overwhelmed. It didn't take Ro long to pack. That same night he packed all his belongings into a small suitcase, which in addition to his portable typewriter, would be his baggage to the "New World."

The next morning he went to the address Mr. Stuart had given him. The receptionist gave him a ticket envelope and wished him a pleasant journey.

An attendant met Ro at the dockside gangway. He looked at the special pass and saluted smartly. "Yes, sir, Mr. Pudaite. Welcome aboard! I'll have the porter get your baggage right away." He motioned for a porter. "Escort Mr. Pudaite to the VIP stateroom and bring his baggage aboard."

Ro offered his small suitcase and typewriter. The porter looked around for the rest. "Is a limousine bringing your baggage?"

"No, this is all I have," Ro answered quietly.

The porter took the two small pieces and led the way aboard. "Follow me, please, sir. I'll take you to your suite."

On deck they walked along a spacious corridor and stopped at a door marked "Stateroom #1." The porter unlocked it and waved Ro inside.

Ro had had no idea what a "VIP suite" meant when Mr.

Stuart had made the provision. It turned out to be magnificent beyond description. Ro was certain a mistake had been made and that they would surely come soon to move him to a lower-class berth.

"This is the entry hall, sir. You can receive your visitors here, and in here is the library." The library had a tall ceiling with a chandelier and wide walls lined with hundreds of books.

"The library also doubles as a dining room, I'm afraid. Hope it doesn't make you feel cramped," the porter apologized.

On the contrary, Ro thought, *even a king could live here luxuriously!* It was finer than any palace or mansion Ro had ever seen.

"And this is your private bedroom suite with bath, sir," the porter concluded, turning on the appropriate lights. Placing the small suitcase on a folding stand, he turned to add, "May I do anything else for you, sir, perhaps polish your shoes?"

The only shoes that Ro owned were on his feet, but he slipped them off and handed them to the porter with a meek thank-you. The porter saluted and left Ro standing in the center of the big stateroom.

A little while later, there was a soft knock at the door. Ro opened it and was greeted by two men. Their attitude was one of profound respect, as if they were addressing the head of state of some nation. The first man, in dark pin-stripes, looked serious and important. The other man, wearing an immaculate, tailored white uniform, saluted smartly.

"Your Excellency," he said, "I am the captain of the ship. And this is the ship's purser. We want you to know that we are here for your comfort and service. If there is anything at all you need, simply ring for us and we'll be at your door."

Ro swallowed and started to speak, but could think of nothing to say.

The captain smiled. "Your Excellency, if you wish to dine alone, simply ring for the steward. But, should you wish to dine in the public dining room, it will be my honor to have you as a guest at the captain's table."

"Thank you. That is most—most agreeable," Ro managed to say.

"Your Excellency. . . ." The captain came to attention, smiled, and saluted.

Ro closed the door and went to the bedroom where he had begun to unpack. Smiling to himself, he thought, *They called me "Your Excellency" as if I were someone important.*

On the bed was his Bible which he had laid out to read before the interruption. As part of his daily Bible reading, Ro began to read where he had left off. The words suddenly came alive and jumped at him:

Behold, what manner of love the Father hath bestowed upon us, that we should be called the sons of God (1 John 3:1).

Ro put the Bible down for a moment to savor the richness of the moment. "Thank you, Lord," he prayed. "I am a child of the King, so you have arranged for me to travel like royalty!" Then he laughed. "Well, since I am a child of God, I may as well enjoy it!"

Ro had made arrangements to travel to Wheaton, Illinois, by way of Canada. He had written Watkin Roberts in Toronto, informing him of his visit. The ship docked a week later in Montreal, Canada.

Ro traveled from Montreal to Toronto by train. The trip lasted far too long for Ro, who was eager to meet the man to whom his people owed so much.

What will Mr. Young Man look like? he wondered. *Will he still remember our people? Will he recall even spending the time in our village? It was so long ago and he stayed just five days.*

When the train pulled into the station in Toronto, Ro took his two pieces of luggage and stepped off on the somewhat crowded platform. He had no idea what Mr. Young

Man looked like. His eyes roved across the people at the station.

Then he heard a voice. "*I dam em? I dam a lawm maw!*" Ro turned, answering, "Yes, I am well, thank you," and then grinned.

"I thought you must be the lad from India. I am Watkin Roberts. This is my daughter, Ruth." He and the young woman both shook Ro's hand. Ruth greeted him in English.

Pu Tlangval ("Mr. Young Man") was no longer young. Ro had imagined him to be a big man with black hair and dark eyes. It was the way Chawnga had always described him. In reality, Roberts was well under six feet tall, and had snowy white hair. He walked with a cane, the result of polio in the thirties. Ro judged him to be in his late sixties. He hugged Ro with the affection of a grandfather.

"I have been praying that at least one of your wonderful people, for whom I pray so much, would come to see me before I die." Roberts spoke several sentences in fluent Lushai, despite the years since he had last used the language.

Roberts, his daughter, Ruth, and Ro drove to the missionary's apartment in Toronto. After refreshments, Roberts and Ro sat looking at each other with obvious joy.

"You know, Rochunga, there wasn't a single sign of civilization when I first came to your area. The people were wild. Your people had chopped off the heads of a lot of British tea plantation workers. The Hmars were the terrors of the Manipur hills. Why, the mere mention of the Hmars and the other tribe—the Bengalis—made everyone tremble."

Rochunga listened and nodded as the soft-spoken missionary continued. "All everyone thought of the Hmars was that they were wild killers. I myself walked through the forests and jungles with fear and trembling. But I knew God wanted me to bring the gospel of Christ to your people.

"I remember that hot summer evening when I first sought permission to enter the Hmar territory. There I sat quite nervously, I must confess, in a straight-back chair in Major

Shakespeare's office. I was a mere lad of twenty-two, but determined to be a missionary!

"'You want to die in a jungle?' Major Shakespeare asked me.

"'Until two years ago—in 1908—I had been a chemist in Wales,' I told the major. 'I had every reason to believe I'd always be a chemist, but then a great revival swept Wales, bringing men to God. It also brought me to God—and to India.'

"'To push your religion on some bloody savages!' the major had argued. 'You do-gooders come out here looking for God-knows-what. Upset the order of things, you do,' he said in a grumpy voice.

"'But the Bible charges us to "go and tell," Major,' I insisted. But, Rochunga, it was all to no avail. Although Queen Victoria was dead, the monarchy and the British Empire still caused the world to shiver out of respect. The Major, who had served under the Queen, held tremendous power. He glared at me for some time."

"What happened then?" Ro asked.

"I simply told him I wanted to contact the Hmar tribe and needed guides to assist me up into the hills.

"'Whose permission do you think you have?' he asked me.

"'I am here by God's grace and I have his permission, sir,' I told him.

"'The Hmar don't fancy visitors, especially ones with white skins!' the Major told me at that point. 'In fact, they're quite likely to chop off your head! We've left them alone since the Alexanderpur tea plantation massacre. They took 500 heads,' he said, 'and it took two columns of Assam rifles to tidy up and teach them a lesson. They've been "out of sight, out of mind" since then.' Colonial policy was absolute on the matter, Rochunga. In fact, I was ordered *to leave the district at once!*"

"How did you first learn of my people?" Ro asked Roberts.

"Well, when I arrived in India, I discovered a book by someone with the same last name as mine, but no relation. The book was *My Forty-one Years in India,* written by General Lord Frederick Roberts. It was full of stories about Hmar headhunters and detailed the tea plantation massacre. I actually felt the hair on my neck stand up as I sensed God leading me to minister to your people.

"I had been in Lushai territory for several months and there translated the Gospel of John into the Lushai language. Then I sent copies of my translation to every Hmar chief in the hills via native runners. A few could read and write in the Lushai language. Lal Kamkholun, the chief in Chawnga's village of Senvon, was the one who had asked the runner to translate the book, but neither the translator nor the chief could understand the meaning. I got word that Lal Kamkholun wanted someone to come and tell him the meaning of the Gospel of John!"

"So that's when you set out across the mountains and my father and his friends heard you singing," Ro said, seeing small pieces of the story fitting together in his mind.

"Exactly. I'll never forget when that warrior threw a spear that landed within inches of me! If the Lord hadn't been with me, I don't know what I would have done." Roberts' eyes grew misty as he recalled the experience. "Then, instead of having my head cut off, I was welcomed as a brother. Their hunger for the gospel was tremendous."

"Yes, it is as my father has told me also," Ro smiled.

"Ah, Chawnga, . . ." Roberts sat back, his gaze drifting toward the ceiling. "Chawnga was a timid young man at first. I once brought him to Aizawl where he spent time in my home learning. He went back to the hills a firebrand. His boldness as a preacher was a gift from the Lord."

"Yes," Ro agreed.

"Your father," Roberts continued, "memorized the entire book of John's Gospel, verse by verse, before going back. Remarkable!"

"Sir, when I was a boy, you were a giant that once walked

our hills," Ro said. "Every leaf in the forest trembled with your name. And when I was older, you—you were a dream that would not go away."

Roberts was obviously pleased. "The Lord has given me this moment, Rochunga. You don't know what your coming here has done for me."

"Why did you leave us, sir?" Ro asked. "Why did you leave India. Your work had just begun."

Roberts looked away, but Ro could see his eyes cloud over. Roberts could not mask the sadness and hurt. He answered without bitterness. "I suppose I 'bent' too many rules by living under the same roof as the tribals and doing things differently from other missionaries. I didn't follow the ways others wanted me to; for example, I encouraged the tribals to preach the gospel to other tribals, as I did with your father. It was a totally revolutionary philosophy—and it got me into a muddle with the other missionaries."

Roberts stood up and hobbled a few steps with his cane, then turned to finish his statement. "I was *expelled.*"

"You could go back. India has independence now and religious freedom," Ro said gently.

Roberts smiled. "The hills of Manipur demand strong legs, Rochunga. Since my battle with polio some years ago, my legs seldom obey me."

The old man looked into Ro's intense face. "Besides, Rochunga, God worked as I knew he would. He commissioned me only to sow the seed. I entrusted the rest to the Holy Spirit. And I was not disappointed."

"Yes," Ro agreed. "Today there are more than 100 churches in the mountains."

The old man looked startled. "So *many?*"

"And your early converts are now our elders and leaders."

"Yes. I want you to tell me how they're all doing."

The missionary walked back to his chair and sat down. "Can you sing me something in your language? Sing just a line."

A little sheepishly, Ro softly sang one of the hymns in

Hmar. Then he translated for the old man: *"The light of eternity has shone in my heart. Do not let me forget that I belong to you, dear Lord. Let me live your life in me."*

Tears welled up in the old man's eyes, and he turned from Ro's gaze. "Please, please try to understand, Rochunga. When I—I was expelled, I went back to my trade as a chemist. And I've always wondered what happened on the mountains when I left forty years ago."

Roberts sighed. "What an amazing Christ!" he exclaimed, his voice cracking with emotion. "He never seeks for our approval, only our obedience and the faith to believe that he is at work when all is mystery."

He leaned toward Ro. "To put one's life in God's hands is not to be led astray, Rochunga," he said. "You see, I was allowed to carry the seed. And you—you, Rochunga, are the firstfruits of the harvest."

Ro blinked back tears. "We have not forgotten you, *Pu Tlangval*," he said. "My father still prays for you every day on the mountain."

"Ah, Chawnga," Roberts reminisced. "Chawnga is still a firebrand for the Lord."

"He is also a rock that will not move," Ro smiled. "My father's firm faith has kept my feet on God's path."

Roberts sat silent for a moment, treasuring the experience. "Yes, Rochunga, the Lord has given me this moment to answer all those years of questioning, doubt, and frustration."

"But, *Pu Tlangval*, how did you come to send me that cable?" Ro asked, explaining that its timing had been providential.

"Well, I have continued to pray for Chawnga, Taisena, and the others. And I've prayed that the Lord would make it possible for my friends, family, and myself to help some Hmar leader come to the West to be educated and trained. I've felt for some time that the day of foreign missionaries in India is coming to a close. If the gospel work there is to continue, it must be under native leadership. One day I heard Winnie Bonar speak. . . ."

". . .Winnie Bonar—from India?" Ro knew the YFC missionary serving in his country.

Roberts nodded. "She was in Toronto to speak and told me about you. When we talked, I discovered, to my great joy, that you were the son of Chawnga. Well, I simply bowed right there in prayer and asked God for wisdom. I sensed the Lord saying, 'This is the man. Send a cable now—send a cable now.' So, I did! And here you are."

"It was God who planned it all," Ro told him, explaining how the Lord had timed the events so precisely.

The two talked for many hours, late into the night, before retiring. Over the next few days, before Ro left for Wheaton College, they would have many more things to share.

Ro and Watkin Roberts ("Mr. Young Man"), the pioneer missionary to the Hmar tribe

ELEVEN
CULTURE AND OTHER SHOCKS

To Ro, from the hills of Manipur, Chicago was a marvelous city. Neon signs flashed and cars honked everywhere. Overhead, elevated trains rumbled like thunder. Buildings towered toward the sky, and people crowded the busy sidewalks, all hurrying to seemingly important appointments. The pace seemed hectic to the Hmar native, but before long, he adjusted.

In the nearby suburb of Wheaton, Ro enrolled in the Wheaton College Graduate School. Wheaton was a pleasant, highly moral community with many friendly faces. Ro soon met a number of American students who welcomed him with smiles and handshakes. In 1955, however, not all the townspeople were as friendly. Some still had provincial attitudes which Ro naively found incomprehensible.

As a graduate student, Ro would have to live off campus, and so he began looking for a room close to the campus. He walked up to one house with a *Room For Rent* sign on the front porch post. A woman answered the door and seemed surprised to see Ro standing there. "Uh—sorry— our extra room has already been rented," she lied.

"No, sorry." The answer was the same at the next house he tried. And the next. It never occurred to him that the rooms were "already rented" because his skin was darker than that of his fellow students.

Finally, however, a jovial American woman cheerfully said, "Yes, I have a room to rent. Would you like to see it?"

"Oh, yes, Mrs. Bartlett," Ro answered.

She showed him the room and explained the terms. "I hope you'll feel at home here, Mr. Pudaite. If there's anything I can do to make you feel more comfortable, please ask."

"Thank you, Mrs. Bartlett," Ro smiled.

He unpacked his meager belongings and arranged his books and study materials on the shelf and dresser of the room. It was small, but cheerful and clean. Most of all, it afforded him the quiet and privacy he appreciated for his studies and translation work.

Ro took time to write to me at St. Mary's College. Our correspondence was to become more frequent and less platonic. Even across the miles, it was obvious that we had a growing affection for one another.

Ro looked for part-time work to help with his expenses. He did all kinds of odd jobs—washing dishes, working in the school library, mowing lawns, weeding gardens, and factory work.

Discovering the ways of the West was as much of an education as his classes. In India, as a boy he had hunted or farmed for food. In the larger villages and in Calcutta, Ro could shop at a marketplace for food to eat. In America, though, he found it strange to see thousands of prepared foods arranged in rows in what the Americans called "supermarkets." At first Ro was overwhelmed by so many choices and spent a great deal of time searching for what he wanted. He was glad that the foods all had colorful pictures on the labels for easy identification.

He wondered what "french-style green beans" were like, but the beautiful photograph of the vegetables on the can label told Ro exactly what they were. He looked at the picture of peaches on another can and put that into his cart.

Next he chose a box of cereal. Ro paused beside cans marked "Sockeye Salmon." The photograph on the label showed a beautiful fish leaping out of the water. He put a can into his cart.

In the next aisle, Ro saw small cans arranged neatly in a row. He took a can and turned it in his hand to see what kind of food it held. There was a picture of a dog on the label. Quickly he returned the food labeled "Alpo" to the shelf.

American slang was also something Ro puzzled over.

"Tha'be all?" the girl at the checkout counter asked.

"Pardon, please?"

"Gettcha some'p'n else?"

"I—I do not understand."

"I said," she spoke more clearly now, "'Is there anything else you'd like?'"

"Oh. No, thank you."

And when one of his fellow students remarked about another, "Oh, you know Ted—he's always chasing girls," Ro wondered why someone would do that and what he would do with girls when he caught them.

Another time a friend named Charlie asked him to meet him at the library at three o'clock. Ro came at the prescribed time and Charlie said, "Ah, you're here. Right on the dot." Ro looked at the floor to see what he was standing on, but saw no dot.

Most of the time at Wheaton College, Ro stayed in his room and studied or worked on the translation. His work of two years filled a thick notebook.

When Ro was well into the second year, his friend Howard Wood knocked at his door. "Ro, I know you're there. C'mon, open the door," he called.

"I'm busy, Howard—translating."

Howard opened the door and poked his head inside the room. "C'mon, Ro, you can't work all the time. What you need is a *date*."

By now Ro knew enough of the way Americans talk to

know Howard wasn't talking about Middle Eastern fruit.

"A date?" Ro asked. "Uh, no, thank you, Howard. I must work."

"Aw, c'mon. Ro. You need to get out of here—relax—enjoy yourself. I've already taken the liberty of arranging a blind date."

"She is *blind?*"

"Uh, no, Ro. I mean—well, I've got you a date with a girl."

"But I have never had a date. In Manipur, customs are different," Ro explained.

"Yeah, I'm sure. Well, listen. Just change your clothes and we'll go, huh?"

"Howard, I would not know how to act. I have never had an American-style date."

"No problem, man. Leave everything to me. There's nothing to it. I mean, we'll go to the girl's house to pick her up. You'll escort her to the car and open the door for her to get in first. Then you go around and get in the other side. At the restaurant, just the reverse. You help her out of the car, escort her into the restaurant, stand behind her when she's seated, and help her with the chair. Then we order. Eat. When it's time to go, you pull out her chair, help her with her coat, walk her to the car, and so on. Nothing to it."

"It sounds simple enough. . . ."

"Good. We'll make it a double date. I'll be there to help you out if you get in trouble. OK?"

"All right," Ro agreed reluctantly.

That evening Howard picked up his date, then stopped by Mrs. Bartlett's house for Ro. He came out and climbed in the back seat of his friend's car. Howard drove to the girl's dorm and pointed to the right door.

"She'll be waiting for you. Just go up, ring the bell, and walk her to the car."

Ro did as he was instructed. A girl answered the bell and greeted Ro enthusiastically. "Why, you must be Rochunga. Ah'm Janet," she said sweetly with a heavy Southern accent.

Janet extended her hand, "Ah'm proud to meet'cha," she said. Ro bowed ceremoniously in the oriental custom.

The girl was nearly six feet tall in her heels and towered above Ro. He had to reach up awkwardly to hold her elbow in order to escort her to the car as Howard had instructed, almost running to keep pace with her leggy strides.

Ro opened the car door and Janet entered the car. He slammed the door, but when he tried to go around the car, he couldn't move. *Why is she holding on to my coat?* Ro wondered. Then he realized it was just caught in the car door. Embarrassed, Ro opened the door, retrieved his coat tail, and shut the door again.

On the way to the restaurant, Janet talked about the hectic day she'd had. "Ah know Monday's warshday back'yonder at home. But Ah've jus' got so useta warshin' on Sati'day that I cain't he'p it. Ah had to wrinch outa coupla things."

Kupla? Ro wondered. *What is a "kupla"?* He made a mental note to look it up in the dictionary when he got home.

At the restaurant, Ro carefully observed as Howard pulled out the chair for his date, then eased it in toward the table when she was seated. Ro tried it, too, but Janet had already sat down. He pushed her chair, but it wouldn't budge. He put his knee against it and shoved with all his might; it still wouldn't move.

The dinner went along without incident, except for his difficulty in understanding his date. During one lull in the meal, Janet turned to Howard. "Ah'm indeed grateful to meetchur friend. He's the cutest thang!" Then turning to Ro, she smiled prettily. "You know that? You don't say much," Janet added. "What'cha skeered of?"

When the girls excused themselves to freshen their make-up, Ro leaned over to his friend and whispered, "Howard, English is a very difficult language. I have studied hard. A little boy in Assam, I study. In Churachandpur, I study English. In Calcutta and Allahabad I study English. In Scotland and now here, I study the English language."

"Yes, Ro?" Howard asked.

"Howard, what language is she speaking? I do not understand *one* word!"

After dinner, the waitress came to take their dessert order. "Would you like ice cream?" she asked.

She started with Ro. "What will you have?"

Ro glanced at Howard, who winked and nodded encouragement. "Go ahead. You start, Ro."

"Uh, well," he looked at the menu for help. "Uh, bring me a chocolate ice-cream cone."

Ro knew he had gone wrong again when the waitress brought three sundaes for the others and set them on small paper doilies. Ro felt like a foolish child licking his cone.

He could hardly wait for the evening to end. To his relief, Howard dropped him off first, then drove the girls home.

The culture shock of Ro's dating trauma lasted a long time. Ro had by then promised himself never to go through such an experience again.

Surely the Lord will find me a wife without the embarrassment of dating! he told himself.

Ro was writing to me more regularly now. He told me of his progress in studies as well as the translation. Although two oceans separated us, Ro and I felt closer to each other than to anyone else. He confided his hopes and frustrations to me in the stream of letters that passed between us. I also wrote to tell him how often I prayed for him. Somehow I was able to help him. "Your faithful and optimistic spirit has convicted me," he wrote. At some low moment in his experience, when he might have wanted to give up, I would write something to encourage and challenge him, renewing his optimism.

Bob Pierce was another encouragement to Ro. The American missionary leader called Ro his "adopted son." When his travel plans allowed or whenever he passed through Chicago's O'Hare Airport, Pierce would phone Ro and arrange to be with him.

"How's the translation coming, son?" he'd ask. When Ro told him, he'd slap him affectionately on the back and smile approvingly. "That's great. When do you expect to finish it?"

"Only a few months remain. I hope to mail the typed manuscript to the Bible Society by summer vacation when school ends," Ro explained.

"You've been working on it a long time," Pierce remarked. "Did you keep track of the time you've put into it, as I suggested?"

"Yes, the nearest I can tell, about 6,000 hours so far."

"Well, let me know when it's done. I'll come and pray with you. We'll dedicate it to the Lord before you send it away."

As the days went by, Ro spent all his waking hours either at work or in class, studying or translating. One day a professor of his called him aside after class to comment on his heavy load.

"You're carrying a sixteen-hour class load, Rochunga, but you're not keeping pace with the class. It's the policy of this school to encourage foreign students, but I'm afraid I can't lower my standards—not even for you," he said. "New Testament theology can be quite demanding, Rochunga. Perhaps you should rethink your program."

"Oh, no, sir!" Ro exclaimed. "I must have every possible knowledge for my translation work."

"Your *what?*"

"I am translating the Bible for the Hmar people in India."

"You are presuming to translate the subtle doctrines of the Word of God for a primitive people? Preposterous! You must stop it at once!"

"B—but, sir," Ro argued. "If I do not do it, who will do it?"

"But you must know Greek . . . Hebrew, . . ." the professor countered.

"Yes, sir. I am working with original languages."

The teacher frowned. Ro continued to explain.

"The Hmar people have had their own language many centuries, but only spoken, never written until recently. The Lord was good—he gave me inspiration. I had an idea to write a grammar primer to help our people."

"A grammar?" the professor repeated.

"Yes. Our people had already discovered that the English alphabet works very well with the Hmar language with some variations. Your *A* became our *Ah*, *B* stays *B*, and so on. This discovery has allowed me to spell almost everything we say with English letters. Our people already use this method."

"And now you're translating the various books of the Bible?"

"Yes," Ro grinned. "Sometimes my head aches with so many shades of meaning to study."

The teacher shook his head.

"Sir," Ro told him, "this book is the only one that can lead my people to heaven. I *must* do it. They must know where they come from and where they're going. Who else will do it, professor. Can *you* do it?"

The instructor bristled. "Such impertinence! Are you trying to humiliate me?"

"Oh, no, sir," Ro apologized. "I mean no disrespect, sir. I merely wish to point out that God has called *me* to do this thing. So, I *must* do it."

The professor frowned, then turned and walked away. Ro watched him, then shrugged in the American manner, and headed toward the library.

TWELVE
WHEN DREAMS COME TRUE

After three years and nearly 7,000 hours of labor, the manuscript was finished. Ro proofread the final verse of the book of The Revelation aloud.

"The grace of our Lord Jesus Christ be with you all!" he cried. An energy and excitement bubbled within him. Ro felt like breaking into a joyful tribal dance and expressing this pent-up emotion as an offering to the Lord.

Not all of his fellow students knew of the accomplishment, but Ro's close friends rejoiced with him that the Hmar translation of the Scriptures was complete. Several met with him to pray before Ro sent the manuscript off to the Bible Society in London. Unfortunately, our beloved "Dr. Bob" [Pierce] was out of the country and so could not be part of that time of dedication.

Several months later Ro began to get galley proofs of the manuscript to proofread and check. Again he was pleased that the project was coming along so nicely. With that major accomplishment done, Ro now wondered about the next steps in his life. Now that he had completed the task to which his father and he had dedicated themselves, what was next?

While he thought about his future, Bob Pierce asked him to participate in World Vision pastors' conferences in Asia.

"The meetings will be conducted in Japan, Taiwan, Singapore, Burma, and India," Pierce wrote.

India! Ro thought. Perhaps he could also visit his wonderful Manipur hills. Ro called Pierce to accept his invitation.

It was difficult trying to study during the spring months while he waited for the summer Asian conferences, but somehow Ro managed. He hadn't realized just how homesick he was for his home, family, and friends. During the time he had worked on the translation, he had usually been too busy to think about home. Now, however, he was often overcome by melancholy.

Ro's mind wandered. He thought about the green jungles and high mountains with the horizons that seemed to stretch to infinity. He remembered the chattering monkeys, the roaring tigers, and the bellowing elephants. How he missed the hills of Manipur!

There was something else. Could one of the biggest reasons for his excitement be that he might also have the chance to visit me at St. Mary's College? Yes.

Summer finally came. The first pastors' conference was held in Japan. Ro shared his testimony with some 1500 Japanese Christian leaders. They were moved by the words of this man, who was an Asian like themselves.

"You were great, son," Bob Pierce said warmly after the meeting. "God was with you tonight."

Ro nodded. He felt encouraged by the warm reception his testimony received. "Yes, and it was because so many of you prayed for me tonight."

"Yes, but *you* encouraged them, Rochunga. You reached 'em in a way we Westerners can't — simply because of our white skins. God is using an Asian to reach fellow Asians. I hope you're sensitive to that, Ro. God might be preparing you for such a ministry."

All the other conferences were just as successful. Their impact touched Ro deeply, and he expressed his feelings of thanks to Bob Pierce for organizing the conferences. The final one was held in Calcutta, so Ro was able to adjust his return trip schedule to allow for a trip to the Manipur hills.

At home Ro received a magnificent welcome. Hundreds came to the village of Sielmat to hear him preach. To the young Hmars, he was something of a celebrity, someone who had actually traveled around the world and back. Wide-eyed, they trailed after him as he walked through the village.

On a previous return home, Ro had organized a "Hmar Bible Translation Committee," headed by a church leader, Thanglung. Ro had asked Thanglung and several of the educated Christian elders from the tribe to help with the translation by checking the manuscript for accuracy. Ro met with them and thanked Thanglung and the others for helping to make the printing of the Bibles a soon-to-be reality.

Before going back to America, Ro decided to postpone his studies. The people of India wanted him to visit villages of the hill tribes and preach. He agreed to a month-long tour.

Ro had two other appointments he wanted to keep while in India. One was a reunion with his happy parents, who joyfully greeted their son. They hadn't seen him in four years and there was much to talk about and share.

The other important trip Ro saved for last—to visit Shillong and see me at St. Mary's College, provided it could be worked into the schedule. That was the hard part. He was all set to make the month-long preaching tour, but getting to Shillong seemed impossible. The tour would begin November 10 and conclude just before Christmas. He had to return to the United States early in January. He could see no way to fit a visit in.

However, the next day, he got a letter from the Bible Society of India, inviting him to a Bible translators' conference to be held November 6–9 in *Shillong! Is this a specific answer to my prayers?* he wondered. "Yes, thank you, Lord," he prayed gratefully.

In Shillong, Ro was busily involved with the conference, but was able to arrange a quick visit to St. Mary's College. A nun received him into the parlor and went to find me.

"You may have five or ten minutes together," she told me as she accompanied me to the parlor.

In the modest, restrained manner of the Hmars, neither of us demonstrated any outward display of affection for each other. Instead, Ro moved toward me and clasped both of my hands in greeting.

For a long while we simply looked into each other's eyes and held hands. Our glowing faces must have betrayed our feelings for each other.

There was so much to catch up on. The "five or ten minutes" stretched into an hour, but the supervising nun did not intervene. Our conversation was laced with gentle laughter and quiet talk.

"I prayed for your work, U Rochunga," I said softly.

"Yes—it was my stength," he admitted. "When I was especially troubled, you remember? I wrote to you. You wrote back and said, 'I too have problems. I do not pray that it will be easy, but that God will give me strength.' Do you remember?"

"Yes," I replied. "I prayed for strength in weakness to do his will, for he said, 'My grace is sufficient for thee.'"

"It was a rebuke to me which I needed," Ro smiled.

"I did not mean to rebuke you, Rochunga," I said, feeling a cloud come over me.

"I know you did not mean it that way, but God used it well. He reminded me that, even as you wrote, his grace is sufficient. Your letters kept me going when I was overwhelmed with work and frustration. It was as if you were with me in person these past years. You could sense my needs."

I smiled and blushed.

"You are one whom I trust with my thoughts," he continued. Embarrassed by his compliments, I could look only at the floor. Ro looked at me with admiration. He had kept my photograph—some four years old now—to remind himself of me. "In the picture you were a schoolgirl. Now I am looking at a woman, Mawii," he said, his face glowing. "I—I came," he stammered, "to see if you might be God's choice—for me to marry, I mean."

Once again I blushed deeply.

"Will you think about it? I must leave India in six weeks. Will you give me your answer soon?"

For a moment I did not answer. Then I told him, "I—I will pray about it."

The next day, after completing his business at the Bible conference, Ro began negotiations, somewhat after the Hmar tradition, in exploring the possibility of marriage.

Two "emissaries" delivered a letter to me. "I will be the happiest man in this hemisphere if God would bring the two of us together in marriage," it read.

I sent back word that I was definitely praying about the marriage proposal. I wanted to tell him my answer in person. For our first date together, Ro invited me to go canoeing on Ward Lake near the Pinewood Hotel where he was staying. It was November, but the weather was unusually clear and warm.

As he paddled lazily across the smooth water, we talked and laughed.

"Mawii, will you marry me?" he blurted out.

I put down the book from which I had been reading to him and looked intently into Ro's face. "I have been praying about it," I answered. "And even as I prayed, instead of asking questions, I found myself praising God for having brought about a miracle."

I smiled shyly. "You see, several years ago, I heard you preach. I told the Lord that if he would have me marry someday, I prayed it would be a man like Rochunga. It was my hope to marry a man who loves God as you do, but I thought it would be someone *like* Rochunga, and not Rochunga himself. It is God's way of answering my prayers, even beyond my hopes."

Ro smiled widely. "Does that mean? . . ."

I nodded yes. "The Lord has made it come to pass. It will please me and make me happy to be your wife, Rochunga—if my parents approve."

Ro's brother, Ramlien, and his brother-in-law, Luoia, acted on his behalf to ask my family's permission for me to marry Ro. There was much joy when Ro got the word: "We are successful!"

Nearly two months later, we were married. The service was held on New Year's Day, 1959, in the William Carey Baptist Church in Calcutta. Reverend Walter Cortlett, Ro's pastor from his student days, performed the ceremony while several church members looked on.

Ro and I stayed in Calcutta our first night together. The next day we took a train to Madras, where Ro spoke at a youth congress. From Madras, we traveled to Vellore where Ro spoke at the famous Christian medical college. Finally, we traveled to Sielmat where Ro introduced me to his family and friends.

Ro's mother beamed when she met me. When she heard how God had brought us together, she said brightly, "Yes, it is *Parthien samsui* ('those whose hair God has braided')," acknowledging God's sovereignty in the marriage.

There was a celebration feast in our honor, besides a delightful surprise for me. "Father!" I exclaimed excitedly. My seventy-five-year-old Hmar father had walked five days through the dangerous jungles to be with me. I wept as I introduced him to Ro. My father smiled warmly and put an arm on Ro's shoulders in blessing. Turning to me, he explained, "Your brothers told me Rochunga was a good man. That is why we sent our permission with Ramlien. They told me Rochunga would be a fine husband. But I had to see with my eyes also." Then he prayed for God's blessing on our new life together.

Ro was deeply touched by this demonstration of love.

"It is most hard for your mother and me to think about our youngest child being grown and going now to the far side of the outside world. It grieves us to think we may never see you again," my father said to me.

Ro explained that he had postponed his leaving for a month. "It will give Mawii a chance to take her final college examinations. And it will allow us to visit Kwawlien village, where Mawii can be a few days with you and her family."

My father smiled brightly. "That will please her mother very much," he said.

Ro and I returned to the United States by way of Toronto. Watkin Roberts met us at the airport, and Ro proudly introduced me as his new wife.

The white-haired former missionary seemed very pleased with me. "You are lovely, my dear," he said. "You'll make an excellent help-meet for Rochunga."

We rested after the long flight from India. "Tomorrow," Roberts said, "I want to have a serious talk with you, Rochunga."

Ro surmised the nature of that conversation. A year earlier, Watkin Roberts had surprised him with a visit to Wheaton when Ro was just completing his translation work.

Mrs. Bartlett had helped Ro set up an office of sorts in an unused corner of the basement of the old house. Here Ro had spread out all his papers and books, and it was here Mr. Young Man had located him.

"Rochunga," Roberts had said to him then, "I'm getting older—over seventy now. I've been praying for thirty years for someone to carry on the work with your people which God saw fit to start with me."

The old man had sat in a straight-backed chair, favoring his polio-crippled leg. He tapped his cane on the floor for occasional emphasis. "A native missionary work can be done best by natives, nationals telling nationals. Ro, I've come here to see if God has said anything to you about this idea."

"I have seen the wisdom of the philosophy you describe," Ro had answered matter-of-factly.

"Rochunga, I want you to pray about taking the leadership of the Indo-Burma Pioneer Mission. True, the organization is almost defunct now. It's all that's left of this old man's dream," Roberts had concluded with a smile.

Ro did not want to disappoint *Pu Tlangval*, but he had no immediate leading from God about this. His main preoccupation for three years had been the translation.

"I want you to take over the mission," Roberts had said.

"But I must finish the translation. Then, I—I do not know what is next. Perhaps in a few years. . . ."

". . . I can wait, Rochunga," Roberts interrupted. "But what about those multitudes of lost Indians? What will happen to the people in the Manipur hills while you wait?"

"I will pray about it," Ro had said finally.

Now, almost a year later, he knew Roberts would be asking him again. In the year since their last meeting, Mr. Young Man had aged considerably, and his health was failing.

As he sat in his own living room, Roberts seemed to carry an additional burden which caused his shoulders to sag even more than usual. "Rochunga," he said, his quiet voice touched with emotion. "You know how much I love India. I've given my life for your people. And, although I was never allowed to go back and live in your village, in my heart I've lived in Senvon since I was a young man—nearly fifty years now."

Ro could not help but be touched with the heart of *Pu Tlangval*, the loving heart of a faithful servant of the Lord God. Images flashed across his memory—images of Chawnga, of the others, of churches planted, of village schools begun, of missionaries and evangelists going out across the Manipur hills. It was all because of one man, a faithful "seed planter" in God's *jhum*.

"My prayers have followed you, Rochunga," the old man said softly. "I have prayed not for myself, nor that you might simply revive an old man's dream. It would be so easy for me to push this responsibility on you, but I don't want to do it. God has to tell you, so I've prayed that God himself would guide your way, Rochunga. I pray that he'll make your way plain, in whatever he wants for you."

"God is making the way plain," Ro said simply. "I know now that he sent you to me last year in Wheaton. Since that time, I have been much burdened by your words to me. As you know, before I left America for India, God led me to take the steps to revitalize the Indo-Burma Pioneer Mission in the United States. Dr. Edman, president of Wheaton College, Dr. Clyde Taylor of the National Association of Evangelicals, and others have agreed to serve as board members. Mawii and I will go back to Wheaton and begin this missionary work for the people of Manipur hills."

The joy in the old man's face was almost too much for Ro to bear. It was a moment of profound meaning for both of them.

The seeds had been planted, watered, and nurtured. New fruit had been harvested, and more seeds planted.

It had been almost fifty years since *Pu Tlangval* had penetrated the jungles and walked over the mountains to the Hmars in the Manipur hills. Then nearly half a century later, Chawnga, the fruit of that planting, was an aging Hmar preacher. He looked toward the mountain where he'd gone to pray during all those years.

Chawnga, now having to lean on his walking staff, had lived for this day. Earlier, wooden crates had arrived from their long journey by ship from London. Inside was a most precious cargo.

"Bibles!"

The people had spread the news across the hills quickly. Hundreds had come to watch as the hardbound books were carefully unpacked.

Tenderly unwrapping one of the Bibles, Chawnga touched it reverently to his lips. Then, eyes brimming, he took it outside and strode toward the mountain. Now, with the first copy of the Scriptures in hand, Chawnga walked up the mountain where he talked with God. The breeze whipped his *puon* and rustled through his loose cotton-spun shirt. At the top, in the smooth, grass-covered clearing, he tossed down his staff and held the Bible in both hands.

Slowly, reverently, Chawnga held the book high as an offering to the Creator God, whose love goes beyond the mountains and encircles even the horizon.

For long moments, the preacher stood and communed with the Lord of heaven. Then, he dropped to his knees in gratitude and began to weep. The emotions of a half century were overwhelming. Devotion, utter joy, worship, and thanksgiving mingled as tears spilled down his cheeks and fell to the earth.

It marked the fulfillment of his dream, his destiny. Yet, perhaps it marked only the beginning of his son's destiny. As an afterthought, Chawnga prayed once again, this time for the path God would have his son, Rochunga, follow.

THIRTEEN
THE TELEPHONE CONNECTION

The initial efforts to revitalize Watkin Roberts' missionary organization were not easy for Ro. Everywhere he went in India, he saw the need not only for schools and churches, but also for clinics and hospitals. He wanted to educate his people to be more productive, to be prepared not only for the hereafter, but for the present.

"Everywhere the Bible has gone," he told a church congregation one Sunday, "blessings have followed. The inventions and good things that have come to the West were because of the Bible. I want my people to find Jesus. But to read about him in the Bible, they must first learn *how* to read and write."

Ro and I spent the next ten years reorganizing the Indo-Burma Pioneer Mission, which later became the Partnership Mission. Under our leadership, more than 300 national missionaries were trained and sent out. About 200 churches were started in northeast India. A hospital, high school, and college were built. The missionary work opened some eighty-seven village schools. In all, thousands of conversions to Christianity resulted from these efforts.

When famine, drought, and floods struck northeast India, Ro responded with an unusual partnership plan. American donors were found to support destitute children in India.

The program was responsible for helping 3,000 youngsters get food, clothing, and an education.

During the same period, God blessed us with three children—Paul Rozarlien, John Lalnunsang, and Mary Lalsangpui—each with an American, as well as a Hmar, name.

For ten years, Mr. Young Man delighted in watching the new work grow. But the former missionary, by now in his eighties, grew weaker and then died.

Ro and I, along with our young children, drove to Toronto from Wheaton. Watkin Roberts' funeral services were conducted by Dr. Oswald Smith, but Ro was asked to deliver the eulogy. He described the legacy of faith, commitment, and devotion *Pu Tlangval* had left behind.

Ro repeated the missionary's words from their first meeting: "'What an amazing Christ! He never seeks for our approval, only our obedience and the faith to believe that he is at work when all is mystery. To put one's life in God's hands is not to be led astray.'"

It was perhaps the sadness of Watkin Roberts' death that initiated Ro's sense of frustration and discontent about this time.

I tried to reassure him. "Why are you depressed? Look at all the Lord has done through you." I reminded him of the unusual growth of the small missionary organization, begun with only a handful of names on a mailing list, with "headquarters" in an old garage at the back of our modest frame home.

After ten years, there had been growth and obvious results in ministry. I read to Ro from one of our brochures, pointing out how many churches, national missionaries, schools, and destitute children had been helped by Partnership Mission.

I left Ro to meditate alone. When I returned twenty minutes later, I said, "Perhaps the problem is not in the task but in the method."

Ro suddenly brightened. "Yes, perhaps you are right.

Let's pray God will give us a way to be more effective in reaching our beloved India."

"We will pray," I said simply.

Not many days later, a strange cable arrived from the Christian leadership in Manipur, where Partnership Mission had its most effective work. They pleaded with Ro to run for a seat in parliament.

As Ro considered the situation, he learned that the Communist who held the parliamentary seat had lost his following and had no chance of political survival. It was certain he could not be reelected. Other potential candidates had met with the Christians and indicated they would not run if Ro returned to India and ran for the seat. A letter explained the situation more fully:

You will only have to file as a candidate. You will not have to campaign at all. Simply come to India in time to file, and you will be assured of the election.

The cable brought exactly opposite reactions from Ro and me. He gave me the wire and watched my eyes widen. "Oh, Ro, it's a wonderful honor!" I said. "Does it not move you to see that they think so highly of you?"

"Yes," he smiled broadly. "It is exciting. Perhaps I should talk with my board members to be certain I have their blessing before going ahead."

"G—going ahead?" I stammered. "What do you mean?"

"Filing—going to India to follow it up."

"B—but, surely you're not! . . ."

Ro looked at me more seriously. "Not what?"

"You aren't really considering it, are you? We would have to give up our work here and return to India."

"We can get help here. And the work is going so smoothly now it can work without my day-to-day involvement. Don't you see? This is the answer to my prayers! God has brought our work to the place where I can be free to pursue something else. I can be more useful in government. Think of the Christian witness I could have in parliament," Ro exclaimed excitedly.

"It is a great honor," I admitted, "but you already have the world's most important job—serving the Lord Jesus. We should be planning how to reach Imphal and all of India with the gospel, not with politics!"

Ro had never seen me so adamant. I broke into tears and left the room. In my bedroom, I wept and prayed.

"Lord," I cried, "I cannot understand this. My heart does not want this. But my husband is so sure. Please give me peace about this so I can be the encouragement to him that I should be."

In his own prayers that night, Ro talked with God about his plans and ambitions. "Lord, you knew I was unhappy and had no challenge. I have prayed for a new vision, something that would have an impact on my world. I believe you have brought this opportunity to me and have been working in our ministry to prepare it for this time."

Then he thought of my concern, knowing I would have to see the wisdom and logic of his opportunity.

"Heavenly Father," Ro continued, "I have peace about this matter. It is what I have always dreamed of. I can see that the time was not right before. Now everything has been prepared, and I am excited. Nevertheless, it is easy for me to follow this path because it is what I desire. But if it is not *your* will, it is a path I do not want to take. Only your will, Lord, do I want."

I had also been praying most of the night. Both of us tossed all night without sleep, our minds heavily burdened.

"Lord," I prayed the next morning, "please give me the assurance that you are leading Rochunga."

"I pray you will give Mawii peace about this decision as you have already given me," Ro prayed.

Everyone with whom Ro talked about the opportunity agreed that it was a wonderful chance to serve God, to be a witness for Christ in the Indian parliament. Ro left for the airport to fly to New Delhi where he had to file as a candidate.

He had decided to give himself plenty of time to get to India and had planned a leisurely trip by way of Moscow. From Moscow, Ro flew to the Russian city of Tashkent near the Afghanistan border, south of the U.S.S.R. The stop at Tashkent would be for refueling only. Then the Aeroflot airliner would fly direct to New Delhi, just a little over 1,100 miles away.

The plane "refueling" stretched to two hours longer than the twenty-five minutes as originally announced. Finally, the flight attendant announced, "There will be a delay for repairs. Passengers will go inside the terminal and be taken to hotels while repairs are made. We expect to take off in a matter of a few hours."

The outside temperature was -25° F. Ro discovered that the hotel room he had been assigned to was not only unheated, but also had to be shared with a drunken passenger. While Ro shivered—fully dressed and still wearing his overcoat and wool cap—his roommate vomited all over the bed.

At dawn the next day, the passengers were taken back to the airport. Once again the plane was delayed. Finally, the plane flew to Kabul in the evening; Aeroflot officials decided to stay over through the night.

Ro began to worry. Although the flight would take only a little over two hours the next day, time was running out. *Tomorrow is the deadline for filing candidacy papers!* he thought, almost panicking.

At 7:00 A.M. Ro left the hotel and hurried to the airport. He went over to the Afghanistan National Airlines counter and learned of a plane going to New Delhi by way of Pakistan. Even by making an intermediate stop in Lahore, Pakistan, he could get to New Delhi in plenty of time.

The flight from Kabul was uneventful, but the Afghan airliner was forced to circle much longer than usual before landing at Lahore. Once on the ground, Ro could see why. India and Pakistan were at war. Pakistani terrorists had hijacked an Air India jet and had blown it up on the Lahore runway.

There was a great deal of confusion and commotion as a few passengers got off Ro's plane. Ro decided to see what was happening. He stepped outside on the top level of the ramp stairway to the cabin door. He stood watching as the huge airliner several hundred yards away was going up in flames. A plume of black smoke towered above the inferno. Instinctively Ro reached for his camera to photograph it.

A Pakistani soldier suddenly ran up to him, grabbed the camera, opened it, and yanked out the film. He asked Ro for identification, and Ro showed him his Indian passport, which alerted the soldier. He immediately took Ro and roughly led him from the aircraft to the airport terminal for a thorough search and interrogation.

A squad of soldiers then boarded the plane. The other passengers were searched and quizzed, but no others were taken to the terminal for questioning. The plane sat on the runway with the passengers waiting while the Pakistani authorities questioned Ro.

When they were convinced of his innocence, they released him. Ro could almost feel the animosity of the other passengers when the plane finally took off several hours later. It landed in New Delhi two hours past the filing deadline.

Khuma and a few other associates met Ro's plane and rushed him to the government offices to see if an exception could be made under the circumstances.

"I am sorry," the official told them. "There can be no exceptions to the deadline. The law is most clear about this."

Khuma and Ro drove quietly to the hotel where Khuma had made reservations. He said nothing to Ro, knowing the deep and crushing despair he must be feeling.

Ro was absolutely exhausted from the events of the past

few days. He fell asleep emotionally numb from the failure to file his candidacy papers.

The next morning, however, was different.

Ro told Khuma, "I have peace. God could have gotten me here in time. But I take it that it was not his plan. He directs my path, and he is pointing to a different way. We must continue to pray. As the Apostle Paul writes in Romans 8:28, '. . . all things work together for good. . . .' The Lord has some purpose even in this."

When I got Ro's cable, I was, of course, relieved that my husband had not been sidetracked from God's calling, *but how disappointed he must be just now*, I thought, wishing I could be there to comfort him.

Back in Wheaton several weeks later, Ro sat at his office desk. That day, for some reason his heart burned with a passion he could not shake. Still frustrated over the inefficiency of efforts to reach the world for Christ, he was praying that God would give him a new plan, a more practical method. After all, if it would take 4,000 missionaries a thousand years just to reach India's millions, what about Africa, South America, and China's *billion* souls?

"Lord, either we must recruit more missionaries, or. . . ." His prayer was suddenly interrupted by a familiar TV jingle.

"Heavenly Father," he resumed, "I pray for a new vision to which I can give. . . ." Again his thoughts were broken by the ringing of the commercial in his mind.

It obviously had to be a "catchy" tune to interrupt his prayers. He realized the jingle was from the Bell Telephone commercial for the Yellow Pages—"Let your fingers do the walking. . . ."

By now, Ro's thoughts were thoroughly interrupted. He opened his eyes. Suddenly, it was as if the almost-audible song in his head became connected to what his eyes saw. Before him, on the desk, were the telephone directories of New Delhi and Calcutta, which he had brought back with him from his unsuccessful trip to file for political office.

A great insight he knew had to be from God hit him. *Of course*, he thought, *telephone books!* Rochunga knew that, unlike America, not everyone in India has a telephone. Only the elite, the educated, the influential had phones. Ro also remembered that these were the leaders of his country. As such, 98 percent of them could read and write English.

"I can use the telephone books as a mailing list and contact all of them personally—witness to them," he told me later as his idea began to develop. "And what better way can I contact them for the gospel than by using God's Word— just as our people were reached over fifty years ago? I will send them a Bible! God's Holy Spirit will be our agent to see that the book is read and understood. He has promised, 'My word shall not return unto me void.'"

As the concept became more clear, Ro reasoned that what was true of India was also good for Pakistan, Burma, and the other surrounding countries. Indeed, could this vision not be used to help evangelize an entire planet? Thus began the Bibles for the World organization.

The vision turned out to be of God—the Lord confirmed it. Ro and I committed our savings—$460—to the project. Others dreamed with us, and soon there was enough money to send over 1.2 million New Testaments to India. We chose a cover photo of the Taj Mahal for the Bibles, entitled them *The Greatest Is Love*, and finally sent them overseas to India's educational, governmental, and cultural leaders.

Housewives and students from various colleges, such as Taylor University, volunteered to type address labels directly from telephone directories of different countries. Retired people, adults, and young people from all walks of life helped package the Scriptures and put stamps on them.

Ro and I had placed a response card and envelope in each book before sending it out. More than 200,000 people from India alone wrote back to say they were reading the New Testament and thanked us for sending them the gifts. Hundreds, if not thousands, were converted to Christianity and wrote to say so. There were scores of *boxes* filled with letters, which Ro shared with missionaries in India for follow-up:

Dear Mr. Pudaite:

Thank you for the beautiful Bible, The Greatest Is Love—The Living New Testament *which I received 19th March 1981.*

It was indeed a pleasant surprise when I got it. I would like to know who sent my name. I hope I will find solutions to all my life's problems in this Bible, which I have started to read. God bless you. . . .

Dear Sir:

I am a Buddhist girl. I received the Bible named The Greatest Is Love *on the first week of July. I have just read this Bible and I want you to know that I have learned a lot about "Jesus Christ."*

I also have peace, comfort, and now know how to live a successful life. Thank you for the book. Thanks a billion!

Dear Pudaite:

I am a young lady who is very much interested to know about the supernatural power, greatest love, Jesus Christ, the truth and the life. Also I have got questions and problems concerning Jesus Christ, peace and everlasting life through him.

You might be surprised how I came to know you but I came to know you through the Bible called The Greatest Is Love *which you sent to my boss. As I opened that Bible in my office, I came across one part on the first page a* note for you *which you showed him how you can help him in all the above mentioned topics. Though the Bible wasn't mine, I happened to be among those longing to get a kind friend from anywhere to share spiritual problems with and also discussions. . . .*

Thank you for your wonderful love and generosity

which is not only realized by me but also to the whole world. May the Lord keep on blessing you. Amen.

About a year into the newly formed Bibles for the World plan, Ro discovered a way to mail Bibles to Russia—legally. Through a friendship pact between Russia and India, cultural materials were allowed to flow freely between the two countries. Ro contacted leaders from Russian missionary organizations in the West to learn which translation of the Bible to use, then printed 50,000 in India, and mailed them to Moscow.

When those Bibles were gone, he raised funds to print another 50,000 and then another. After 100,000 of the Russian Bibles had been sent, Ro sent representatives to Moscow to verify whether they were actually getting through or were simply being confiscated as some of his critics had charged.

Independent checks determined that the Russian people were indeed getting the Bibles through the mail. Some even wrote asking for additional copies. The few, if any, which were confiscated by authorities would be read also, since Bibles are in high demand on the Soviet black market.

Bibles for the World quickly became Ro's obsession. "We know God's Word has the power to change men's lives. And when lives are changed, so are the destinies of nations, and perhaps even the world," Ro told his board of directors.

He now clearly understood his new mandate from God: give God's Word to the world's more than four billion people—most of whom have never seen a Bible or New Testament.

As with the horizon Ro had watched as a boy, the horizon of humanity never stands still. The number of telephone subscribers has been growing rapidly. By 1990, an estimated *one billion* telephones will be in use around the world.

"I want to ignite the whole world with the Word of God," Ro tells audiences when he speaks today. The strategy definitely works. As with Watkin Roberts, the pioneer missionary who went off the beaten track to bring God's Word to a place previously bereft of it, so Ro's mailing of Bibles is sowing the same seed in places closed to conventional missionary efforts.

Ro presented a plan to his board to give a Bible or New Testament to one out of every five people in the world before the end of the century. In order to send one billion copies of the entire New Testament—about one copy for every family on earth—Ro plans to enlist the help of Christians worldwide. Some can be prayer warriors; others can provide financial resources. Still others can organize Bible packing and mailing events for their churches, youth groups, or fellowship groups. Businessmen and individual families could mail one Bible a day.

Ro calls this practical and exciting plan of Bible mailing "Operation St. Paul." It is a program in which every Christian can participate. No one is too young or too old, too poor or too rich to play a part in this program. With this strategy, every Christian can become a "missionary" and every church a "world mission center."

God has already prepared the way for countries to receive his living Word—through the international postal system. There are more than five million postal carriers worldwide. Ro says they act as "missionaries" and deliver the Bibles through ordinary mailing routes!

So far, we have mailed over six million Bibles and New Testaments, blanketing entire countries such as India, Taiwan, Burma, and Rhodesia.

As expected, Ro's efforts have not been without problems. We have been attacked both by the forces of Satan and even by some Christian organizations which have actively opposed Ro's dream. And, as before, God has proved faithful in showing his superiority over the powers of darkness and petty jealousies. Miracle after miracle—in funding, timing, and results—has proved the Lord's inspiration for the plan.

Scriptures in Farsi (the Iranian language) were mailed to

Iran at the height of the U. S. hostage crisis. Before Russian troops invaded Afghanistan, that country was provided with Scripture from Bibles for the World. A special bilingual English-Chinese edition (similar to Mao's little red book of quotations) is currently being sent into Mainland China.

And so, the seed planting goes on. . . .

A personal word to you from the Author:

Perhaps you would like to be involved in the work that God has entrusted to Rochunga Pudaite. You can help send Bibles and New Testaments to people who otherwise might never read the Word of God.

Write for information on how your church, Sunday school class, or business can obtain Bibles or New Testaments to mail. Bibles for the World will supply the Scriptures, wrapping materials, and addressed labels at cost. You or your group wraps the Bibles, affixes the labels, and buys the stamps to mail them from your home, church or business.

Help as the Lord leads and enables. Your contribution, regardless of the amount, will help accomplish this enormous task. All contributions are tax deductible.

Write to:

Dr. Rochunga Pudaite
Bibles for the World
P.O. Box 805
Wheaton, IL 60187